Over the eleven years we have known David MacDerment, he has shown an exceptional skill in revealing Scriptural truths in a soli' and tand-able manner. While we were Deans of the Institute of M stian Retreat, David's teachings on finan the anointing of the Holy Spirit fed the stu no matter their age or spiritual experien me-times were "milk," they quickly turned t tne talk" attitude will rub off on you as you progress throu * *is "training by covenant." Start now to walk by the covenant professed in this outstanding book and you will be brought to a new, and exceptionally higher, level of understanding of your covenant with God.*

—Robert and Dolores Balla,
Former Deans, Institute of Ministry
Ministers and Elders, Fisherman's Net Revival Center, Venice, Florida

This is a book "for such a time as this," when we as believers need to focus on Covenant living rather than culture conditioning. With tongue-in-cheek humor, the author may push your buttons and intrude on your comfort zone, but you'll be motivated to "grow up!" and enjoy the benefits of God's super-natural power in your life.

—Joanne Derstine, writer and speaker
Christian Retreat Conference Center, Bradenton, FL

I have known David MacDerment for many years, and highly respect him as an articulate Bible teacher knowledgeable on any Bible subject. He has been on the faculty of our Institute of Ministry at Christian Retreat for many years, and I consider this man of God to be among our nation's top Spirit-filled theologians. David's unique style always captures the attention of our students as he uses practical and often humorous illustrations to convey the truths brought forth. His teaching is not always "comfortable," as it prods us to higher levels of faith, but it always points us to the Savior and urges us to realize who we are in Christ.

Cultural Nonsense will excite and fulfill the hunger and thirst in Christian seekers looking for mature, honest answers in their walk with God. Allow this book to be a part of the rest of your life.

—Gerald Derstine, D.D.
Chairman of the Board, Gospel Crusade, Inc.
Founder and Director, Israel Affairs International (IAI)

I'm passionate about Cultural Nonsense *the latest book by my friend, David MacDerment.*

Impacting our world for the cause of Christ is not just a good idea—it's a divine directive. Our success in promoting Kingdom principles is attributable to an inner commitment and faith that must be both unmovable and unshakable.

In his powerful book, David gives us a roadmap to discipleship far more detailed than anything you could ever find with MapQuest. Sadly, our mental hard drives are being programmed by popular culture instead of the rules for success in life found in the Word of God.

Cultural Nonsense *is a call to arms. Do yourself, your family and your friends a favor, don't just read this book once. Read it again and again so that you and those you know and love will be strengthened and nurtured through this anointed teaching.*

I highly endorse Cultural Nonsense *and believe it will be an agent of change for those believers who're serious—really serious about changing their world.*

—Harold Herring
President, Debt Free Army and Millionaire University
Rich Thoughts Television Network

Refuse to be Unteachable!

For everyone who continues to feed on milk is obviously inexperienced and unskilled in the doctrine of righteousness (of conformity to the divine will in purpose, thought, and action), for he is a mere infant [not able to talk yet]!

But solid food is for full-grown men, for those whose senses and mental faculties are trained by practice to discriminate and distinguish between what is morally good and noble and what is evil and contrary either to divine or human law. (Hebrews 5:13,14) AMP

CULTURAL NONSENSE

CULTURAL NONSENSE

DON'T BUY THE LIE OR SETTLE FOR LESS THAN BLESSED

DAVID MacDERMENT

REAL WORLD TRAINING FOR THE BELIEVER

Oviedo, Florida

Cultural Nonsense—Don't Buy the Lie or Settle for Less than Blessed
by David MacDerment

Copyright © 2009 David MacDerment
All rights reserved

Published by HigherLife Development Services, Inc.
2342 Westminster Terrace
Oviedo, Florida 32765
(407) 563-4806
www.ahigherlife.com

ISBN 13: 978-1-935245-12-4
ISBN 10: 1-935245-12-0

All Scriptures, unless otherwise noted, are taken from the King James Version of the Bible.

09 10 11 12 13 — 8 7 6 5 4 3 2 1

Printed in the United States of America

DEDICATION

Making a book dedication is an interesting concept.

How do I properly acknowledge credit to someone
for a quality contribution they made into my life?

My Mom for birthing me?

My Dad for letting me live with them so long?

My precious wife Beverly for her patience,
tolerance, encouragement, and proof reading?

To my friends in the ministry, some of whom
have been down the trail before me?

To my many ministry partners for their
inspiration and loyalty and support?

To those dedicated covenant trainers who have been sharing
their anointing to teach the Word to me for all these years?

To the Holy Spirit for His leadership into truth?

Well, the answer is *yes* to all. Many, many thanks to all those
listed above as well as a few others. Thanks for helping
me to be a vessel for God to use to bless the people.

TABLE OF CONTENTS

INTRODUCTION

The Bible is filled with stories of great events. In both the old and new covenants (the Old Testament and New Testament of the Holy Bible), God chooses seemingly ordinary people and very unusual circumstances to accomplish spectacular feats. This divine intervention into the lives of men and women has inspired countless readers over the ages.

But what about you? And what about now? Can we have the faith to believe that God will continue this pattern of involvement in our lives? Are you seeking a closer understanding of God and his workings? Do you want to see a real demonstration of his power released into your life in a truly personal way?

If you've answered yes or are even a little curious, then the New Testament training contained in *Cultural Nonsense* is for you.

David MacDerment has given his life to helping believers come to a life-long conclusion that the presence and power of a loving

God is personally available to them every single day. His passion is to see believers biblically trained so they can live life by their covenant with God—not by today's culture. It is our choice to live life here empowered by the Holy Spirit of God or exist on the fringes of faith without accessing heaven's power. Victory is accessible to us!

Many of the advantages of this world's cultural systems are limited to special groups. In the things of God, there are no restrictions based on age, gender, race, ethnic background, or socio-economic status. Any believer on the threshold of discovery can learn to overcome spiritual and natural challenges here on earth. God's plan is to offer you a relationship and participation with him. It's for YOU in the HERE AND NOW.

Cultural Nonsense deals with the power of the personal ministry of the Holy Spirit in the life of a believer. The author's objective is to train the Christian to apply the things of the Spirit to his everyday life and take his place as the conqueror over life's challenges.

Blended with humor and a unique view of life on earth as only David MacDerment can provide, the material is presented in a sometimes confrontational "in-your-face" style of teaching which demands a decision from the reader. Which horse are you going to ride? The author uses varied and powerful approaches to present Bible truths which evoke laughter, tears, discomfort, and even anger—but result in great encouragement and confirmation that our God is on our side and is prepared to manifest his presence in our everyday lives.

The teaching lessons in *Cultural Nonsense* are uniquely practical. This real world training is based on a Bible study course entitled, Practical Anointing, which the author has presented to students and audiences for over fifteen years.

Refuse to be unteachable!

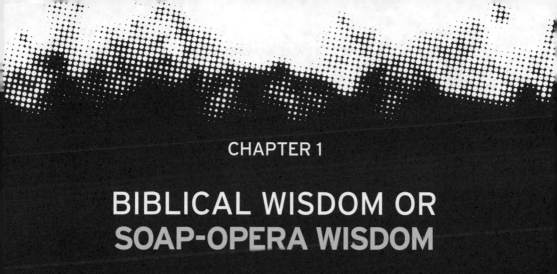

CHAPTER 1

BIBLICAL WISDOM OR
SOAP-OPERA WISDOM

They just don't know any better." Perhaps you've heard someone say these words about another person's behavior: this may be true! Our eyes and ears are the outward gates and channels to our mind and our spirit man. If all of the information that a person permits through his eyes and ears has been a lie, is it any wonder his reasoning is filled with lies? When he opens his mouth, that's what comes out.

If people let soap operas through their eye gates and ear gates, then soap-opera wisdom is what will come out of them! If people let the Word of God through their eyes and ears, the Word of God is what will come out of them.

Let me share a personal example (and this is a "Beverly-approved" story):

A while back, my business schedule required me to travel back and forth from Miami to Los Angeles, making two or three round trips each week.

About a month into that routine, my day was progressing fairly typically. Out on the 6:00 a.m. flight from Miami, change planes at Houston, fly on to Los Angeles, grab the rental car, off to the big office tower, sit in the business meeting, review the reports, eat the brought-in and catered lunch, never leave the boardroom table, interview the guy with the new plan, discuss the details with the principals, negotiate the fees and project out the costs, off to another boring dinner meeting, deal with more business aggravations and incompetent people...are you getting the picture ?

At the end of a series of very long and tedious eighteen-hour days, I was finally back at the hotel, headed for my room. When entering the elevator, I still had enough energy to smile at my fellow riders and maintain a general pleasant demeanor. Quite frankly, I really didn't notice any particular features of the people, only that one of them, an attractive woman, smiled back. Exiting on my floor, I made my way along the hall till the right room number appeared.

Just as I slipped the key into the lock, a most pleasant female voice from behind me said, "I can see you're tired—would you like me to come in and rub your back?"

As I turned around to see the source of this offer, all kinds of alarm bells and whistles were going off inside me. My spirit man instantly knew the correct answer to the question—NO! My mind knew the correct answer to the question—NO! It wasn't even a close call, no protracted debate. The temptation was right there, but so was the force of righteousness built up in me over the years of seeking God, submitting to his word, being led by his spirit.

The answer from me was immediately, "No, thank you." And I went directly into my room and closed the door.

Now here's the point of the story. Everybody in this deal gets a vote. Spirit man votes no. Mind votes no. But how do you think my flesh wanted to vote? I am laughing out loud as I write this. My flesh was screaming, presenting the information my mind had to consider to make its decision.

A back massage? Secret sex? Are you kidding me? Soap-opera wisdom? My flesh says that sounds like a great idea! But a life-long battle, a process, if you will, brings and keeps my flesh and yours under subjection. The old man is truly dead. Don't let him try to wake up again! Even Joseph knew when to run!

Besides risking the health of my physical body from sexually transmitted disease, improper sexual contact would be a clear violation of the marriage covenant I made with my God and my spouse. You see, I didn't have to make the decision to be faithful that night in the hotel. I made the decision to be faithful to her the day we got married. And what is more important, it would be disloyal to the God in whose name we made that marriage covenant. True Christian marriage is not just a marriage of one man and one woman. It is a holy union between those two family members and their God.

I reinforced my correct decision by immediately calling my wife back in Florida. I told her exactly what happened. Honor requires transparency.

Men and women have a God-given, built-in mechanism to be drawn to each other. Handled properly, this God-given desire results in lifelong fidelity within a marriage. Handled improperly, we have a husband looking at something improper on his computer or a wife flirting with an office worker. If it gets to this point, the battle has been lost in the mind, and ungodly behavior may soon be the victor.

In the natural realm, your eyes and ears are the receivers God gave you to collect information upon which you can base your decisions. But as Christians, we are no longer like "mere men," as Paul states:

And we also [especially] thank God continually for this, that when you received the message of God [which you heard] from us, you welcomed it not as the word of [mere] men, but as it truly is, the Word of God, which is effectually at work in you who believe [exercising its superhuman power in those who adhere to and trust in and rely on it]. (I Thessalonians 2:13 AMP)

The resolution between those conflicting pieces of information (what the flesh wants and what the Spirit of God wants) takes place in the mind or soul. I like the way my sister and ministry partner Joyce Meyer puts it when she describes the soul as the location of the battleground. It is in this personal battleground where the decision-making takes place for your life. Each piece of information, regardless of the source, is available for your consideration, decision, and action. Jesus taught us that out from this abundance in your spirit man you will speak words.

When the man or woman of God sows the Word of God (which means you read, listen to, think about, and speak the Word of God), that good word is a direct deposit in the mind and spirit man of the hearer. When an ungodly man or woman sows an ungodly word (such as anger, strife, gossip, hatred, or soap-opera wisdom), that word is also a direct deposit into the mind and spirit man of the hearer.

For out of the abundance of the heart the mouth speaketh. (Matthew 12:34)

Your words are a reflection of your abundance. Think about what comes out of your mouth the most—words of faith or words of fear, doubt, and unbelief. Are you speaking the truth or a lie? Light or deception? Confidence or doubt?

We are truly new creations who have never walked the earth before—with full-time residence of the Holy Spirit and led by the power and anointing of the Word of God. The difference between the believer and other human beings, who are also members of the creation of God, is the indwelling presence of the Holy Spirit.

The Holy Spirit is the receiver God has given you to collect revelation from the Father upon which you can base your decisions and actions. He is a direct contact to reveal to you the will of the Father—heaven's wisdom delivered directly to you.

In other words, in addition to your <u>eternal</u> spirit temporarily living in a body with a soul, the believer has the added advantage of the witness of the Spirit of God. Only believers have this witness available to them—no one else—no animals, no unbelieving humans (heathens), and no other so-called religions. The availability of the personal ministry of the Holy Spirit of God is the exclusive territory of the Christian believer.

So we are not limited to those things which enter through our eyes and ears. One of the benefits of membership in the family of God is that we can develop our communication with the Holy Spirit, who lives within us. This is powerful revelatory knowledge, which is far superior to mere information available from the senses.

Can you see that even the finest, morally minded man with a wonderful secular education will always be at a distinct disadvantage when compared to a believer who has the personal witness of the Holy Spirit? And I'm not talking just about those delicate, moral issues which are popular to the church. Our revelatory knowledge includes things about our everyday lives such as marriage, career, self-government, finances, and personal ministry.

Every true believer must gain this unique perspective to function well in God's supernatural kingdom. We are not natural beings who have had a spiritual experience. We are eternal spirit beings who are having temporary, natural experiences down here on this earth.

Because we are members of Christ's body, we are to be careful what we allow to enter into the eye gate and ear gate.

> And he said unto them, Take heed what ye hear: with what measure ye mete, it shall be measured to you: and unto you that hear shall more be given. (Mark 4:24)

I speak on the subject of living by covenant almost every week of the year. I kid around and tell my audiences, "This is a no-milk meeting!"

The New Testament writers speak of an initial level-of-faith-and-covenant-training called the milk of the Word. It's where we all start after joining the family of God. And just like after a person's natural birth, this milk provides the new believer with his or her first scriptural meals. Milk deals with the basic preliminary truths of our faith. These truths provide the foundation for all the New Testament covenant training which should follow.

But that's where the trouble starts. Believers are encouraged to press on past this MILK level and get into the real meat of the Word. Unfortunately, some of us have been weaned on a shallow review of milk-level information in a short twenty-minute class on Sunday morning. That's not true Bible study. Most believers avoid the time and effort required to do any in-depth study of critical topics of covenant which really affect their lives. They just let the pastor do all of their homework for them. They show up once a week to get spoon-fed and omit the dedicated individual study that produces real life-changing faith.

Limited Word produces limited revelatory knowledge and limited personal impact. Believers in general have greatly underestimated the necessary labors in completing this assignment of divine service.

NO MILK simply means that we are prepared to make that commitment of time and desire, to immerse ourselves in the Word on a given topic, and to press on until that which we study manifests in our lives; not just to seek after the things of God in some academic pursuit, but to see the fruit of His heart of goodness and our commitment.

If you're in the mood for a tender, juicy steak, you're in the right class—in this case, you're in the right book! But what about you? Are you interested in putting worldly, soap-opera wisdom into your eye gates and ear gates, or are you longing to live your life according to biblical wisdom? Are you ready to leave the milk of the Word and take some savory bites of a marinated steak hot off the grill? If that's you, then read on! Let's look at the skin we live in, the world we're part of, and what influences us in our day-to-day existence on this planet.

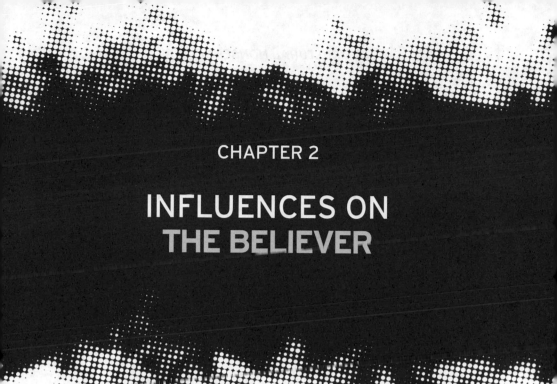

CHAPTER 2

INFLUENCES ON THE BELIEVER

S atan is the enemy of your soul. Satan has a lot of tools he uses to entice you into considering his false wisdom and information:

- demons
- devils
- low-level spirits
- curses
- hindrances
- fear
- sickness
- poverty
- death
- lies
- deception

- bondage
- burdens
- yokes

What a list! Can you identify with any of these tools of entice-
ment? Day after day, ever since your birth, the enemy of your soul
has attempted to use every available delivery system to deceive,
distract, and draw you away from the truth and the source of all
truth.

> *In whom the god of this world hath blinded the minds of them
> which believe not, lest the light of the glorious gospel of Christ
> [The Anointed One and his anointing], who is the image of God,
> should shine unto them. (II Corinthians 4:4)*

THE god OF THIS WORLD

The world, too, has ganged up on you, and since the majority of
the world's institutions are run by the god (small "g") of this world,
is it any wonder that most of the information we receive is based
on lies and deception? All we need to do is look at the outcome of
most people's lives (judge them by their fruit) to see that they have
based many of their important decisions on defective information.

Based on a rough census, the population breakdown of the
earth is currently along these lines: Using the loosest definition
of *Christian*, there are approximately one billion-plus Christian
believers on earth. We'll agree to use a definition which declares
some level of recognition and allegiance to Christ. The other five
billion people are outside of the family, do not enjoy the membership privileges of the church, and by their very spiritual position
are denied the witness of the Holy Spirit and divine revelation.
They are part of God's creation but not part of his family. They
have gotten the most basic, the most all-important question of all
time wrong: *What are you going to do with Jesus?*

Can you see why we as believers need to make a dedicated focus on world evangelism? Five out of six don't know Christ, and that is far too many people to miss heaven. They are simply the children of the wrong father. Sounds familiar, doesn't it? Isn't that what Jesus told them? He said that if you don't recognize me it's because we have different fathers, and your father is the devil. Pretty powerful words!

> Jesus said unto them, "If God were your Father, ye would love me." (John 8:42)

> For whatsoever is born of God overcometh the world: and this is the victory that overcometh the world, even our faith. (I John 5:4,5)

Have you ever given any thought to that Biblical promise of overcoming the world? Exactly what aspects of the world have you overcome?

> And the devil, taking him up into an high mountain, shewed unto him all the kingdoms of the world in a moment of time. And the devil said unto him, All this power will I give thee, and the glory of them: for that is delivered unto me; and to whomsoever I will I give it. (Luke 4:5,6)

First, we need to answer two quick questions to make sure we're on solid doctrinal grounds:

1. What did Satan offer to Jesus?
2. How did the devil ever end up in a position to possess it and be able to offer it?

The answer to the second question should be clear even to a basic-level student. The dominion over the earth given by God the Father to Adam in the Garden of Eden was stolen by Satan through subterfuge and deception. Adam lost his authority by making the wrong decision about who to believe, God or the snake. Since

Adam relinquished his allegiance to God and chose to believe the devil, man's dominion was lost and transferred over to Satan— that is, until Jesus came down here and regained it for us.

If you've gotten that piece of truth settled in your mind, let's press on with question number one: What did Satan offer to Jesus? What exactly are these kingdoms of the world over which Satan retains authority?

> The Latin term is Cosmos (sometimes spelled "Kosmos") Diabolicus, which is defined as *all of the world's system (kingdoms) which Satan offered to Jesus.* It includes economic, political, educational, social, and man-made religious systems that operate and control this world. These systems, for the most part, have been developed by man to conform to the ideals, aims, and methods of Satan. The total success of these demonically inspired systems is in large part attributed to an insidious integration of satanic principles throughout each of the various kingdoms.

In many instances, nonspiritual, carnally minded men unknowingly further the devil's goals in the promotion of governmental, financial, and educational pursuits. Often those men are clearly influenced by seducing and deceiving spirits, and have no clue what's really going on.

The believer definitely has unchallenged and undefeatable authority in these areas of Satan's stolen dominion, but that authority is totally based upon one's revelatory knowledge, following the leadership of the Holy Spirit, and obedience to the Word of God. Remember, it's not even a close fight between our God and his empowerment of us against the devil and his forces. The believer's supernatural abilities and authority (the anointing) are God's impartations to us which permit us to overcome the world (Cosmos Diabolicus), which our Jesus has already defeated.

> *I have told you these things, so that in Me you may have [perfect] peace and confidence. In the world you have tribulation and*

trials and distress and frustration; but be of good cheer [take courage; be confident, certain, undaunted]! For I have overcome the world. [I have deprived it of power to harm you and have conquered it for you.] (John 16:33 AMP)

He that committeth sin is of the devil; for the devil sinneth from the beginning. For this purpose the Son of God was manifested, that he might destroy the works of the devil. (I John 3:8)

INFLUENCE OF THE FLESH

And then we get to the influences in the natural realm—the flesh. These are quite easy for us to understand—painfully easy. The wrestling match which takes place in the mind on many occasions is prompted by input from the natural, fleshly realm. Those carnal influences combine with our senses and heredity to bombard our souls with sensory input.

Now before I get so spiritually minded and become no earthly good, let me say here and now that some of these fleshly sensations are wonderful blessings from God...a walk in the mountains on a spring day, tender, intimate relations with a spouse (I mean good, biblically legal sex between a married man and woman), a delicious porterhouse steak cooked just the way you like it, a good night's sleep, a dip in a cool stream on a hot afternoon. These are all good and precious sources of natural input. But some natural input is ungodly.

After every meal, the mind has a decision to make. Our flesh thinks it's a perfectly reasonable idea to eat a quarter of a pie and a quart of ice cream after every meal. As far as flesh is concerned, there is really nothing to decide! No debate is needed, and the mind should forget all about this battleground speech. As far as flesh is allowed to influence and convince the mind in this area, the weight and dimensions of a believer's earth suit will soon get out of balance. Oh, I'm sure none of your clothes are arranged in the closet based on time and size!

Let me tell you a short story which will demonstrate the power of flesh messages. (By the way, this is a "Beverly-approved" story.) I'm in the grocery store, intently reading the information label of some product, oblivious to all other activity around me. A lady walks past me, and in her wake is a cloud of a perfectly intoxicating aroma, some delicious fragrance that has absolutely and instantly captured the attention of my flesh information receivers.

In an instant, before my preoccupied mind has even a split-second to consider what has just happened, out of my mouth comes, "Don't you smell good?"

Thank God, the lady did not hear me, or if she did, she never looked back but went on walking down the grocery aisle. I stood there in near disbelief. Within the blink of an eye, sense realm information had bypassed my conscious mind and was delivered out loud through my mouth. I was so embarrassed, I didn't know whether I should run out of the store or hunt down the woman in the ketchup aisle and apologize. It was better to just let it go, but it was a valuable learning experience. The sensation was so powerful and so immediate that it startled me to see how quickly it made it through the loop—in the nose and out the mouth!

Now, before you start laughing so loud that the neighbors will hear you, are you sure nothing like that has ever happened to you? Is everything that comes out of your mouth always a product of prayerful, holy, spiritual deliberation?

Our lifetime walk of faith is a continuous awareness of the struggle between flesh and spirit and making the correct godly choices. The holy goal is to crucify the flesh and be led by the Spirit of God.

Can you see the process? Can you see the spiritual principles involved? Why do you think Paul has to tell us to keep our flesh under subjection?

> *But I keep under my body, and bring it into subjection: lest that by any means, when I have preached to others, I myself should be a castaway. (I Corinthians 9:27)*

For You have put everything in subjection under his feet. Now in putting everything in subjection to man, He left nothing outside [of man's] control. But at present we do not yet see all things subjected to him [man]. (Hebrews 2:8 AMP)

Do you see the sources of the influences on the believer? Think about the chart. Just like the climax of those old-time western movies, it's about time to bring in the cavalry. Look at all the power on God's team. The Father, the Son Jesus, the Holy Spirit, his angels, anointed ministers, the Word of God (in 17 translations), the truths of his covenant, power, might, the anointing, forgiveness, mercy, redemption, gifts, health, healing, provision, abundance, the force of faith, and the list goes on and on. What a package! What a deal! What a God!

Many years ago, when I was in vocational-auto-shop class in high school, the instructor used a simple teaching tool called a cutaway. It was a cross-section of a Chevrolet V8 engine. This plastic model revealed the internal working parts of the engine and had a simple electric motor and battery that made it rotate to demonstrate the moving parts.

Instead of trying to imagine what was happening beneath those vibrating metal covers on the engine, we could physically see what was going on with each part in its proper position in relation to the other. As the pistons moved up and down and the crankshaft turned, it was easy to observe what was happening inside the engine.

While the popular cutaway demonstrates what's inside the V8 engine, the diagram pictured here illustrates what's going on inside this very complex piece of equipment called *us*. I've been told that one of the most expensive and necessary tools for students in medical school is a life-size model of a human body which has plastic and rubber internal parts, all in their proper position and in relationship to each other. I can only imagine how much easier it must be to be working on the real thing if you've had an opportunity to work on the model first.

Look at the various sources of those influences as they are depicted on the diagram, Influences on the Believer #1.

What you see in this illustration on the next page is an artist's rendering of the believer, a cross-section or cutaway. Just imagine that we have taken the average believer—let's call him Uncle Al— freeze-dried him and sliced him vertically so we can see how he works and what he looks like inside.

In our examination of the influences on a believer, the first question we must answer is, ***What is a believer?*** We have been told that we are made up of three parts:

1. An eternal spirit being
2. A natural body
3. A mind or soul

For the word of God is quick, and powerful, and sharper than any two-edged sword, piercing even to the dividing asunder of soul and spirit, and of the joints and marrow, and is a discerner of the thoughts and intents of the heart. (Hebrews 4:12)

SPIRIT

The eternal spirit being is what we're really all about! Our spirit beings were created by God and destined to live after the physical body ceases to live. The evangelist has properly taught that your spirit being will live after your physical death, either in one place or the other depending on your choice—your personal acceptance or rejection of Jesus Christ.

We know that the natural, physical body is temporary. It has been attributed to the late Rev. Kenneth Hagin who described the body as our "earthsuit." Just as the astronaut needs a specially designed spacesuit to wear in outer space, our spirit beings need a natural earthsuit to operate down here during the time we are here. The body provides the mechanism we need in order to

INFLUENCES ON THE BELIEVER

I have a soul (mind)

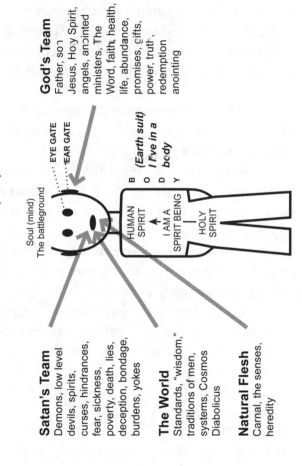

God's Team
Father, son
Jesus, Holy Spirit,
angels, anointed
ministers, The
Word, faith, health,
life, abundance,
promises, gifts,
power, truth,
redemption
anointing

EYE GATE
EAR GATE

Soul (mind)
The battleground

(Earth suit)
I live in a
body

B
O
D
Y

HUMAN
SPIRIT

I AM A
SPIRIT BEING

HOLY
SPIRIT

Satan's Team
Demons, low level
devils, spirits,
curses, hindrances,
fear, sickness,
poverty, death, lies,
deception, bondage,
burdens, yokes

The World
Standards, "wisdom,"
traditions of men,
systems, Cosmos
Diabolicus

Natural Flesh
Carnal, the senses,
heredity

temporarily house our eternal spirit being, our mind (or soul), and it provides mobility. Our physical body was given to us by God so that we may relate effectively to the natural realm.

The mind is a slightly different matter. Just as the body is subject to change by sickness or health or conditioning or movement, the mind also is subject to change. I'm not just talking about changing our minds about what's for dinner tonight. Rather, I'm referring to the significant changes in the mind's ability to comprehend and apply new information, to discern different circumstances, and to learn how to make decisions which will produce different results for our lives.

Most animals relate to the natural world quite well in their environment. Contrary to popular politically correct thinking, there are major differences between us and the animals. Animals are able to learn by a conditioning during repetitive acts of behavior. We've all seen the chimps and gorillas on the science shows pointing to the TV screen and selecting the appropriate answer symbol for a repeated question and receiving the banana. And we've seen some unsaved spiritually blinded scientific type draw the massive conclusion that the monkey is within one or two lessons of being elected to Congress! But really, are you ready to send a monkey or a porpoise into town to negotiate *your* next real estate deal?

Of course, there are obvious physical differences between mankind and the animal kingdom. Mankind possesses a higher mind or intellect, is made in the likeness of God's image, and possesses an eternal human spirit. The eternal destiny of the spirit (heaven or hell) is determined by the decision the mind makes concerning Jesus Christ.

Now I like monkeys and I like cows (some cow parts are especially good on the grill). I like birds and all the neat fish and colorful bugs God made, and every living thing which reflects his creativity, his genius, and his unlimited abilities to manipulate the natural realm. But I'm not going to marry one or expect it to balance my checkbook! Animals were put on earth to meet the needs of the people God created. Humans are placed in authority and at the top of the food chain. The herb-roasted chicken on my rotisserie does not deserve to have a court-appointed attorney and a public hearing before it is cooked and eaten. Should animals be needlessly abused? Of course not. Nothing in the natural realm should be needlessly abused, but keep in mind that animals are here to be used by us for our benefit, need, and pleasure.

MIND (SOUL)

Paul gives us stern instructions concerning our obligation to renew our minds with the word of God. (You may refer to a later section titled *Renewing Your Mind*.) Jesus tells us what goes on in our minds can be dangerous and warns us about what we allow through the eyes and the ears. They both are talking about the great struggle in the mind for the believer—whether to be taught by the culture or taught by the covenant. Why do you think the enemy is so relentless in bombarding the culture with his deceptions?

Sometimes it appears to me that the enemy and his followers understand Mark chapter four better than most believers. When presented with a lie over and over again, some humans begin to believe the lie. If you don't think that's true, consider what we have been told during the election cycle and just watch the TV campaign ads.

Keeping that repetitive principle in mind should help you come to a clearer understanding of why the world's systems are demanding to be the sole source of information you receive for you to consider. Secular media, TV, so-called "news," junk science, public institutions, opinion polls, social theory, and political spin doctors are all targeting your mind.

Things such as individualism, homeschooling, Bible study, strict adherence to constitutional law, debt-free lifestyle, principled dissent, self-reliance—these things will not be tolerated in their opposition to the world's systems. That's what is really behind politically correct oppression.

> *But while men slept, his enemy came and sowed tares among the wheat, and went his way. (Matthew 13:25)*

> *He said unto them, An enemy hath done this. (Matthew 13:28)*

> *The enemy that sowed them is the devil. (Matthew 13:39)*

You are either trained by the culture or trained by the covenant.

CHAPTER 3

WHAT IS THE ANOINTING?

I am so eager to talk to you about the anointing in your life! God is so good. Despite all the influences that come against the believer, he has given us the way to overcome!

Now before we dive into this top sirloin, may I recommend to you a few "steak knives" to help you get the most out of this teaching? Read over this quickly or absorb each detail in the following small section. Whatever you do, find, beg, borrow, or obtain by faith the following study tools:

RECOMMENDED STUDY TOOLS

1. King James Version of the Bible

Many newer versions of the Bible will offer a variety of other language presentations and study aids. Some may be easier to read. However, only the use of the original *King James Bible* will offer the largest selection of additional study aids, not the least of which is *Jim Strong's Concordance. Strong's Concordance* doesn't work with any of the other translations. Should you choose to neglect the *King James Bible*, you will lose out on a powerful study aid. With every word numbered, defined, and cross-referenced for both Hebrew and Greek translations, this magnificent aid will enhance your ability to study and find the heart of God in the scriptures.

2. An Older Version of *Webster's Dictionary*

Do your best to find an older version, perhaps before the mid-1960s (before they threw God out of the public schools).
 Why go through the trouble of finding such an old dictionary? Look at this example: Check out the word *covenant.* These older editions defined "covenant" as "God's agreement with his people." In most newer additions, all references to God have been purposely omitted by the heathen cultural elite.

3. *Jim Strong's Exhaustive Concordance*

This thing is as big as the Philadelphia phone book! You can generally get the paperback edition on sale for less than $20. There is simply no better resource material available than this concordance. It is imperative for a better understanding of both the ancient Hebrew language as well as the Greek. For example, if you do an in-depth study of the word *faith*, you'll learn that having faith has an implication of an adventure.

4. *The Amplified Bible*

Although the ancient English King James version had excellent Hebrew manuscripts available to the translators, the best Greek texts for the New Testament did not arrive for use by the translators until more than ten years after the King James translation had already been completed. It is my sincere personal belief that no true student of the Word of God can be as effective in his studies without regularly using a copy of *The Amplified Bible*. If you do not have one, RUN, do not walk, to the nearest Bible bookstore and get yourself a copy of *The Amplified Bible*. Many times in class I will ask my students if they are still suffering under the serious spiritual disadvantage of not having an Amplified Bible among their resources.

Of course, I don't want to make a statement like that without providing an example, so let me show you just this one:

> *If any man come to me, and hate not his father, and mother, and wife, and children, and brethren, and sisters, yea, and his own life also, he cannot be my disciple. (Luke 14:26)*

Hate your mom and dad? Hate them? Let us allow the Amplified Bible to clarify this for you:

> *If anyone comes to Me and does not hate his [own] father and mother [in the sense of indifference to or relative disregard for them in comparison with his attitude toward God] and [likewise] his wife and children and brothers and sisters—[yes] and even his own life also—he cannot be My disciple. (Luke 14:25 AMP)*

Oh, I see. All of my earthly relationships I must view with relative disregard when compared with my relationship towards God. Did that help? Just get yourself an Amplified Bible and see what else it will do for your spiritual understanding.

5. Complementary Translations

I use a large variety of complementary translations such as *The New King James Bible, The Living Bible*, and others as my study aids. They provide for me great additional study resources and sometimes unique insight into the true meaning of the word, phrase, or topic.

Your personal study resources are important for the fulfillment of your spiritual destiny. When the Apostle Paul was imprisoned, he recognized the importance of his own study materials when he sent for his books. You can tell a little bit about how serious a person is about Bible study by which resources get taken on a trip or vacation. Another indicator shows up when you do your financial books at the end of the year.

The hand of the diligent tendeth to plenty. (Proverbs 21:5)

As you are listing all of the various expenses and making your totals of housing, food, car expenses, ministry expenses, etc., notice what was spent for the study tools needed for YOUR walk of faith. How much did you spend for books, CDs, computer software, and Bible seminars?

If you want the real protein, what Paul describes as "the meat of the Word," then get ready! There are some savory bites of marinated steaks presented in the following pages.

WHAT IS THE ANOINTING?

In a broad sense, the anointing is the supernatural, divine intervention of God into the natural realm. But who exactly is involved in the anointing? We need to look at the anointing, what it is, what it does, and who can participate.

First, let's look at those who <u>receive</u> the benefits of the anointing.

Scripture after scripture describes situations where people outside of the body of Christ have been favored and blessed with receiving the powerful benefits of the anointing. The king received supernatural wisdom from the mouth of Daniel because of a specialized anointing to interpret dreams.

Forasmuch as an excellent spirit, and knowledge, and understanding, interpreting of dreams, and shewing of hard sentences, and dissolving of doubts, were found in the same Daniel. (Daniel 5:12)

When Jesus healed the two demon-possessed men of the Gergesenes, he demonstrated a transfer of the anointing directly from the Anointed One into the spirit, soul (mind, will, emotions), and body of people who were without reason, out of control, dangerous, and completely driven by demonic spirits.

> *And when he was come to the other side into the country of the Gergesenes, there met him two possessed with devils, coming out of the tombs, exceeding fierce, so that no man might pass by that way. (Matthew 8:28)*

> *And when he went forth to land, there met him out of the city a certain man, which had devils long time, and ware no clothes, neither abode in any house, but in the tombs. (Luke 8:27)*

> *Because that he had been often bound with fetters and chains, and the chains had been plucked asunder by him, and the fetters broken in pieces: neither could any man tame him. (Mark 5:4,5)*

By the way, this same demonic spirit is frequently found and promoted in the advanced training in Oriental martial arts classes. Our demonically influenced culture has become very effective at recruiting; that's their form of evangelism.

Under the guise of developing personal discipline, physical fitness, or so-called "self-defense" classes, countless thousands of parents blindly send off their young children to be placed under the influences of Eastern religions (demons). There they learn to draw on that "special power" they have down inside them.

Just exactly WHO put that special power in there? You parents better get real and figure out what power you want your kids to possess and draw on. And they make it so easy. Why, they'll even pick up your kids in a van after school, take them to karate class, drop them off at home, and let you charge the costs on your credit card or offer convenient financing terms.

> *And always, night and day, he was in the mountains, and in the tombs, crying, and cutting himself with stones. (Mark 5:5)*

(Today police, social workers, and public school counselors report cutting and self-mutilation are increasing at an alarming rate among demonically influenced young people.)

Then the Anointed One spoke a word of deliverance. Look at the results that the transfer of the anointing brought about in the possessed:

> *Then they went out to see what was done; and came to Jesus, and found the man, out of whom the devils were departed, sitting at the feet of Jesus, clothed, and in his right mind: and they were afraid. (Luke 8:35)*

Delivered by the Word of God! Studying the Word of God and in his right mind! That was and still is a powerful word for a guy like me!

> *They also which saw it told them by what means he that was possessed of the devils was healed. (Luke 8:36)*

When God brings about that kind of dramatic change in your life, people will talk about it.

A unique anointing was available to Moses—a specialized "opening bodies of water" anointing. As he raised his staff, the Red Sea opened. Look at all the people who benefited from that specialized anointing :

> *And Moses stretched out his hand over the sea; and the LORD caused the sea to go back by a strong east wind all that night, and made the sea dry land, and the waters were divided. And the children of Israel went into the midst of the sea upon the dry ground: and the waters were a wall unto them on their right hand, and on their left. (Exodus 14:21,22)*

We need only to look at Pharaoh and the heathen people of Egypt and ask them if they had ever seen evidence of the supernatural anointing.

> *And I have also heard the groaning of the children of Israel, whom the Egyptians keep in bondage; and I have remembered my covenant. Wherefore say unto the children of Israel, I am the LORD, and I will bring you out from under the burdens of the Egyptians, and I will rid you out of their bondage, and I will redeem you with a stretched out arm, and with great judgments. (Exodus 6:5,6)*

In your own study time, examine how the plagues on Egypt had NO NEGATIVE EFFECTS on the covenant people of God because of the protective anointing of their Father. (Refer to Exodus chapters 7 – 12.)

- Our guys' snakes ate their guys' snakes
- Waters turned into blood
- Frogs appeared in abundance
- All the dust of the land turned into lice
- Swarms of flies
- Heathen cattle and livestock had bad sickness

(BUT nothing shall die of all that is of the children of Israel)

- Boils upon every Egyptian man
- A grievous storm of hail and fire destroyed their guys, their crops, and their livestock

(BUT only in the Land of Goshen where the children of Israel were was there no hail)

- Locusts covered the face of the earth to finish off what the hail did not
- Darkness in all of the land of Egypt

(BUT the children of Israel had light in their dwellings)

- The death of the first-born of Egypt

(BUT seeing the blood on the doorpost, the destroyer passed over)

Look how God described His covenant of protection in the Psalms:

> *A thousand shall fall at thy side, and ten thousand at thy right hand; but it shall not come nigh thee. Only with thine eyes shalt thou behold and see the reward of the wicked. Because thou hast made the LORD, which is my refuge, even the most High, thy habitation; There shall no evil befall thee, neither shall any plague come nigh thy dwelling. (Psalm 91:7-10)*

WHO DISTRIBUTES THE ANOINTING?

Genesis, the book of beginnings, shows the creative anointing of our God in his divine ability to speak and create. The Word of God is anointed to bring itself to pass:

> *For as the rain cometh down, and the snow from heaven, and returneth not thither, but watereth the earth, and maketh it bring forth and bud, that it may give seed to the sower, and bread to the eater: So shall my word be that goeth forth out of my mouth: it shall not return unto me void, but it shall accomplish that which I please, and it shall prosper in the thing whereto I sent it. (Isaiah 55:10,11)*

We should be coming to a basic conclusion that the power of the anointing is above the power of the natural realm. It is truly "super" natural or above the natural. Our great God the Father is the source of all natural law. By his creation and by his regulation, the planets remain in their orbit, the tides rise and fall on a regular schedule, the earth turns, and the sun appears to rise and set.

And yet we see another side of the totality of God when the flesh-and-blood man Jesus of Nazareth walks on water:

> *And in the fourth watch of the night Jesus went unto them, walking on the sea. (Matthew 14:25)*

Doctrinally speaking, this ought to give us some food for thought regarding spiritual power dominating over natural power. Any alert student remotely familiar with the laws and principles of the physical sciences should observe that this is highly irregular. You should also see that this suspension of natural law was not universal, in that the laws of gravity and buoyancy were not universally suspended worldwide, but the unique experience was only focused on those of faith at a given point in time and location.

I suppose we should not be surprised or amazed that our Father, who is the source of all natural law, would reserve the right to suspend or modify those laws according to his will. What is amazing, however, is that he would delegate that authority to flesh and blood (us).

> *Ye are of God, little children, and have overcome them: because greater is he that is in you, than he that is in the world. Hereby know we that we dwell in him, and he in us, because he hath given us of his Spirit. For whatsoever is born of God overcometh the world: and this is the victory that overcometh the world, even our faith. (I John 4:4,13; I John 5:4)*

Ken Copeland speaks of the definition of the anointing in this way: it is the power of God on flesh doing what flesh cannot do by itself.

God, through the lips of Isaiah, foretold the coming of the Anointed One. Isaiah tells us in the tenth chapter and the twenty-seventh verse that at the appearance of the Anointed One burdens shall be removed and yokes shall be destroyed because of the anointing.

> *And it shall come to pass in that day, that his burden shall be taken away from off thy shoulder, and his yoke from off thy neck, and the yoke shall be destroyed because of the anointing. (Isaiah 10:27)*

Properly translated from the Greek, Christ means the Anointed One.

Every place you read Christ in the New Testament, it refers to one of its four meanings:

1. Jesus, the flesh-and-blood man from Nazareth
2. The coming Messiah
3. The Anointed One
4. The anointing (the power and force)

Wherever the word **Christ** is found in the scriptures, translate and meditate on the appropriate meaning(s).

You cannot separate the Anointed One from the anointing. If he is in you and you are in him, you have become part of the anointed. You are "a little anointed one." "An anointian." " A Christian."

Because of The Anointed One, I am An anointed one.

> *And when he had found him, he brought him unto Antioch. And it came to pass, that a whole year they assembled themselves with the church, and taught much people. And the disciples were called Christians* [little anointed ones] *first in Antioch. (Acts 11:26)*

What did they teach? The disciples testified of what they witnessed.

> *The word which God sent unto the children of Israel, preaching peace* [wholeness, completeness, nothing missing, nothing broken] *by Jesus Christ* [the Anointed One and His anointing]: he is Lord of all): *That word, I say, ye know, which was published throughout all Judaea, and began from Galilee, after the baptism which John preached; How God anointed Jesus of Nazareth with the Holy Spirit and with power: who went about doing good, and healing all that were* <u>oppressed</u> *of the devil; for God was with him. (Acts 10:36-38)*

THE LUKE 4 CHECKLIST

Jesus gives us a "checklist" for the anointing, shows us what it will do, and declares that the earlier prophecies have now come to pass:

And Jesus returned in the power of the Spirit into Galilee: and there went out a fame of him through all the region round about. And he taught in their synagogues, being glorified of all. And he came to Nazareth, where he had been brought up: and, as his custom was, he went into the synagogue on the sabbath day, and stood up for to read. And there was delivered unto him the book of the prophet Esaias. And when he had opened the book, he found the place where it was written, The Spirit of the Lord is upon me, because he hath anointed me to preach the gospel to the poor; he hath sent me to heal the brokenhearted, to preach deliverance to the captives, and recovering of sight to the blind, to set at liberty them that are bruised, To preach the acceptable year of the Lord. And he closed the book, and he gave it again to the minister, and sat down. And the eyes of all them that were in the synagogue were fastened on him. And he began to say unto them, This day is this scripture fulfilled in your ears. (Luke 4:14-21)

Look at that word *oppressed* from Acts 10:38, and then see what Isaiah says:

*And all thy children shall be taught of the LORD; and great shall be the peace of thy children. In righteousness shalt thou be established: **thou shalt be far from oppression**; for **thou shalt not fear**: and from terror; for it shall not come near thee. (Isaiah 54:13-17)*

In Isaiah 11:1-2, Isaiah tells us what the Anointed One and his anointing will do:

And there shall come forth a rod out of the stem of Jesse, and a Branch shall grow out of his roots: And the spirit of the LORD shall rest upon him, the spirit of wisdom and understanding, the spirit of counsel and might, the spirit of knowledge and of the fear of the LORD. (Isaiah 11:1,2)

Think about the names of the Spirit of the Lord and the specific empowerment he imparts:

- The Spirit of the Lord
- The Anointed
- The Spirit of Wisdom
- The Spirit of Understanding
- The Spirit of Counsel
- The Spirit of Might
- The Spirit of Knowledge

For God hath not given us the spirit of fear; but of power, and of love, and of a sound mind. (II Timothy 1:7)

Forasmuch then as the children are partakers of flesh and blood, he also himself likewise took part of the same; that through death he might destroy him that had the power of death, that is, the devil; And deliver them who through fear of death were all their lifetime subject to bondage. (Hebrews 2:14,15)

Since, therefore, (these His) children share in flesh and blood— that is, in the physical nature of human beings—He (Himself) in a similar manner partook of the same (nature), that by (going through) death He might bring to nought and make of no effect him who had the power of death, that is, the devil. And also that He might deliver and completely set free all those who through the (haunting) fear of death were held in bondage throughout the whole course of their lives. (Hebrews 2:14,15 AMP)

Him we preach and proclaim, warning and admonishing every one and instructing every one in all wisdom, in comprehensive insight into the ways and purposes of God, that we may present every person mature—full grown, fully initiated, complete and perfect in Christ, the Anointed One. (Colossians 1:28 AMP)

So that we may boldly say, The Lord is my helper, and I will not fear what man shall do unto me. Remember them which have the rule over you, who have spoken unto you the word of God: whose faith follow, considering the end of their conversation. Jesus Christ the same yesterday, and to day, and for ever. (Hebrews 13:6-8)

I can do all things through Christ [the Anointed One and his Anointing], which strengtheneth me. (Philippians 4:13)

When Jesus came into the coasts of Caesarea Philippi, he asked his disciples, saying, Whom do men say that I the Son of man am? And they said, Some say that thou art John the Baptist: some, Elias; and others, Jeremias, or one of the prophets. He saith unto them, But whom say ye that I am? And Simon Peter answered and said, Thou art the Christ, the Son of the living God. (Matthew 16:13-16)

REMEMBER YOUR DEFINITIONS! CHRIST EQUALS THE ANOINTED ONE!

And Jesus answered and said unto him, Blessed art thou, Simon Barjona: for flesh and blood hath not revealed it unto thee, but my Father which is in heaven. (Matthew 16:17)

There is a perfect insight into the personal witness of the Holy Spirit, revealing that which is unavailable through natural sense-realm information.

And I say also unto thee, That thou art Peter, and upon this rock I will build my church; and the gates of hell shall not prevail against it. (Matthew 16:18)

By the way, in case some of you denominational-types have been exposed to a doctrine whereby your religion's leader is supposed to be an actual bloodline descendant of Peter, the rock, please consider this alternative meaning to this verse: Jesus is merely stating that he will build his church on the faith-filled relationship of supernatural, revelatory knowledge provided by the Father's Holy Spirit directly to any believer. In any event, let's not get into a denominational war over it.

And I will give unto thee the keys of the kingdom of heaven: and whatsoever thou shalt bind on earth shall be bound in heaven: and whatsoever thou shalt loose on earth shall be loosed in heaven. (Matthew 16:19)

To more fully understand the principles of binding and loosing, study the upcoming chapter on spiritual authority.

So then faith cometh by hearing, and hearing by the word of God. (Romans 10:17)

Can you sense the faith coming to receive the anointing building up in you?

But ye have an unction from the Holy One, and ye know all things. But the anointing which ye have received of him abideth in you, and ye need not that any man teach you: but as the same anointing teacheth you of all things, and is truth, and is no lie, and even as it hath taught you, ye shall abide in him. (I John 2:20, 27)

This doesn't invalidate Ephesians 4:11, which includes a teacher in the five-fold public ministry. Rather, this refers to that internal witness of the Holy Spirit that "something is wrong here" when you are exposed to lies and false doctrine. We certainly need that special gifting in today's world!

Ye are of God, little children, and have overcome them: because greater is he that is in you, than he that is in the world. Hereby know we that we dwell in him, and he in us, because he hath given us of his Spirit. For whatsoever is born of God overcometh the world: and this is the victory that overcometh the world, even our faith. (I John 4:4,13; I John 5:4)

Thank God for the personal indwelling presence of the Holy Spirit!

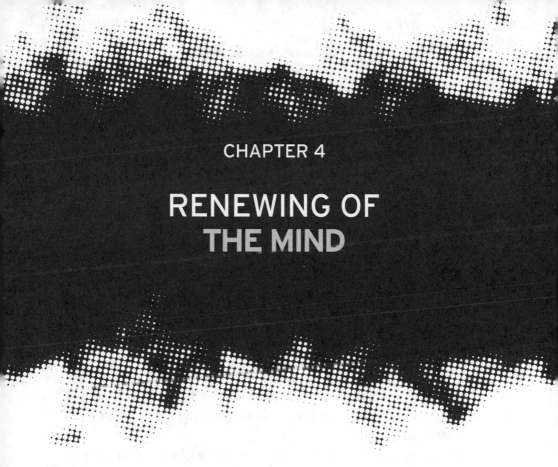

CHAPTER 4

RENEWING OF THE MIND

W e can experience the anointing of God in our everyday life! God not only wants to invade the natural with his supernatural presence, but he actually enjoys hanging around with us. There is nothing sweeter than day-by-day fellowship, friendship, and partnership shared between me and my God. That's what Adam and Eve had with the Lord when they walked with him in the cool of the day in the garden. For a period of time they did obey God—and they also discussed things with him and talked about everyday life, sharing friend to friend. It's hard to imagine anything better! Even though I know there's nothing sweeter, nothing more fulfilling, my mind still argues against that anointed lifestyle. Sometimes it can be a battle.

Your soul (or mind) is a compilation of experience, knowledge, and sensory inputs. It's composed of intellect, emotions, skills, habits, learned experiences, spiritual influences, training, inclinations, discipline, dispositions, morals, standards, fears, faiths, obsessions, priorities, memories, plans, and more.

> *Do not be conformed to this world (this age) [fashioned after and adapted to its external, superficial customs], but be transformed (changed) by the [entire] renewal of your mind [by its new ideals and its new attitude], so that you may prove [for yourselves] what is the good and acceptable and perfect will of God, even the thing which is good and acceptable and perfect [in His sight for you]. (Romans 12:2 AMP)*

Now just imagine your mind as an egg carton with those separate little compartments. What's in each compartment has a source, an origin. Some are godly, some satanic, some worldly, and some fleshly. If you can grasp this and recognize that you are in charge of what gets in those little compartments, you are in a better position to change what is in there, make better decisions, and get better results.

Jesus taught us to guard what goes into the gates or doors of our eyes and ears:

> *And he said unto them, Take heed what ye hear. (Mark 4:24)*

The process of renewing your mind involves replacing the contents of the containers with godly things and getting rid of the ungodly things. Remember, you are either trained by the culture or trained by the covenant.

Here's another good place to clearly understand Mark 4, where the sower sows the word:

> *And these are they by the way side, where the word is sown; but when they have heard, Satan cometh immediately, and taketh away the word that was sown in their hearts. (Mark 4:15)*

The Soul (mind)
THE EGG CARTON *Before Renewal*

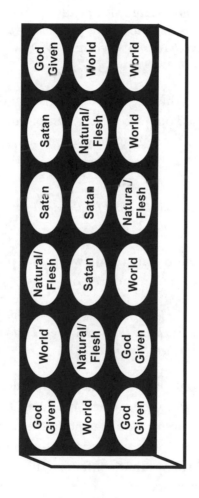

The soul (mind) is comprised of intellect, emotions, skills, habits, learned experiences, spiritual influences, training, inclinations, dispositions, morals, standards, fears, obsessions, priorities, memories, plans, and more.

And these are they which are sown among thorns; such as hear the word, And the cares of this world, and the deceitfulness of riches, and the lusts of other things entering in, choke the word, and it becometh unfruitful. (Mark 4:18,19)

Then the cares and anxieties of the world and distractions of the age, and the pleasure and delight and false glamour and deceitfulness of riches, and the craving and passionate desire for other things creep in and choke and suffocate the Word, and it becomes fruitless. (Mark 4:19 AMP)

Don't give place to the devil. That means you don't give him a place to stand beside you, talk to you, tempt you, accuse you, or sow his seeds into your ear gates or eye gates.

Neither give place to the devil. (Ephesians 4:27)

Leave no [such] room or foothold for the devil [give no opportunity to him]. (Ephesians 4:27 AMP)

Don't give the devil or any of his workers a place to sow seed into your life. Submit your mind to God.

Cause me to hear thy lovingkindness in the morning; for in thee do I trust: cause me to know the way wherein I should walk; for I lift up my soul unto thee. (Psalm 143:8)

If any of those containers are filled with a demonic influence (demon, unclean spirit, etc.), which produces manifestations of Satan's hellish kingdom in your life and in the lives of others, you and/or your fellow believers can employ the anointing power of the Holy Spirit to clean out that container. That eviction process is called spiritual deliverance.

The ancient King James English calls it casting out devils. Whatever you call the process, it is definitely not uncommon for a believer to have picked up a stray devil or two somewhere along the way. Sometimes they were invited in on purpose, depending on your choices of lifestyles, friends, spouse, your personal sin selections, or beliefs.

Oh, I know that some people think they've picked up a devil like you would catch the flu at the state fair, by accident or casual contact. Hardly. All they have is a bad case of spiritual ignorance.

After all, deliberate sin is considered as a cause, another cause for demonic influence to arrive, stay, and influence a believer's life is ignorance—the absence of truth. Many believers just haven't sought out the proper New Testament training in how to resist the devil. They missed the class on spiritual authority. There is an ultimate liberty and personal freedom in taking spiritual authority and dominion over the devil's influences in your life.

> Submit yourselves therefore to God. Resist the devil, and he will flee from you. (James 4:7)

One translation says he will run away in stark terror. He has no choice when faced with the authority of the Word of Jesus, the Name of Jesus, and the Blood of Jesus. How rewarding it is to know that God has empowered each believer with the same potential as Jesus demonstrated when he confronted Satan head-on.

Let's not get carried away with seeing a devil behind every thought. Some are, most are not. Much false information promoted in our culture as truth has a demonic source but often is not a direct result of demonic possession of or influence on an individual. What all this deception does show us is that so much of what we have learned is based on the falsehoods of the systems of this world, which are run by the god of this world.

Here are some examples:

Thinking that smoking cigarettes is cool or sexy or a right of passage at a certain age is more cultural deception. For a person to be chronically addicted to tobacco or any other drug over long periods of time is probably evidence enough to suspect demonic influence and the need for spiritual deliverance, as well as the ministry to the physical body.

While we're on this point, don't underestimate the power of the truths found in the chapter on spiritual authority. Natural forces do not triumph over spiritual forces. To expect certain self-destructive patterns of behavior to be conquered by natural means only, without using spiritual deliverance, is fantasy. All you need to do is examine the results of all those secular self-help programs which are designed to operate without God or his Word or the power of the Holy Spirit (the anointing).

Young people's concept of self-worth that is based on their fashion selections or use of certain slang words to be "in" are other examples of cultural deception. However, self-degradation and criminal acts as initiation requirements for a fraternity or social club may have a demonic influence.

One powerful demonic influence which is manifesting in today's popular culture is the mutilating and marking of one's body. I am simply amazed at the number of so-called Christian parents who blindly allow their children to be cut or pierced or permanently marked to conform to some perverted cultural standard or peer pressure coming from other similarly misguided and unsupervised youth. In just a few short generations, these barbaric practices have become commonplace.

All one needs to do is open one's eyes at any public gathering and observe the sheer number of young people with exposed arms, legs, backs, necks, and more who are permanently ink-marked. This mindless submission to the advice of unknown spirits (unknown to them) is characteristic of demonic influence. Young men, especially, have willingly allowed themselves to be marked with heathen tribal symbols and writings of pagan religions.

Honestly, is barbed wire a sign of freedom? They have unknowingly agreed to be marked for the devil and his forces. It is an open invitation, whether they know it or not. The believer exercising the gift of spiritual discernment should know better. These markings are as much of an invitation as playing with witchcraft. It is a point of contact in the spirit realm for a demon. They serve the same purpose as the jack-o-lantern on All Hallows Eve. It is a traffic signal, a directional control.

I recently saw a dramatic transition take place in a teenage boy. He was a typical American high school boy, interested in cars and sports, working regularly part-time, a fairly reliable, responsible young man. He was being raised in a lukewarm, non-Spirit-filled Christian home with very weak New Testament covenant training, but they did manage to show up in church every few Sundays.

In a matter of weeks, the young man was dressed in black and was cut and pierced in multiple locations with shiny polished metal objects stuck through the new holes, including his tongue. Did I mention what color his hair was? When I saw this finished "work of art," it was in a business setting where he was coming in to pick up his paycheck. I was unable to contain my comments.

"Do you know you have just locked yourself out of most of the attractive career options you had?"

"Can you understand that the personnel director of the company where you're applying for that upscale job is going to have the same reaction to you as I am having?"

"Can you honestly expect to be taken seriously looking like that?"

"What employer in his right mind would let you represent his firm or make decisions for his business when you obviously are unable to make sound decisions for yourself, even at the most basic physical levels?"

"For a young man, you have not only marked your body, you have marked your life and your future."

"I hope you don't expect much out of life financially because you have just locked yourself into a low-paid labor job for life. You'd better get comfortable in it—that is, unless you can get a job in a tattoo parlor or a freak show. But forget dealing with the public or in a professional position."

The young man was given his paycheck. He wasn't fired immediately; he was still allowed to operate company equipment and do lower-skilled labor chores. Previous to this transformation, he was on track to assume a beginning management responsibility over a work crew, but not any more. The company will make no further attempts at his technical training, and will limit his exposure to customers, suppliers, and other valuable business contacts. He wasn't alienated from his family. Believers still invite him to church activities in some desperate hope that he will change and straighten out.

Perhaps you think my response seemed harsh. You have a point, and I'll allow for that and repent where appropriate. But sometimes a dramatic response is needed to a flagrant situation which has been allowed to progress unchallenged by people who just don't know any better. Sadly, this poor, misguided youth hadn't been taught the truth about this form of deviant behavior early on or, for that matter, taught about many other things that will have major impact on his life. His parents left most of his real training up to the culture and his peers. The result was evident.

This massive spiritual problem is occurring on a daily basis among many well-meaning yet spiritually lukewarm Christian families. The sad outcome is a direct result of low Word level. Serious New Testament covenant training is completely absent from the daily routine. Public school, the internet, Hollywood movies, and television have been the primary sources of wisdom. Since the family leadership never bothered to take Bible study seriously, Mom and Dad know little of the principles of Biblical economics and covenant wealth management.

The new bass boat and furniture have taken precedence over tuition for a good Christian school. The annual expenses for games, videos, and secular or cultural music can't be reduced to spend money on Bible study aids or attend a training seminar. And since the family has never really participated in God's plan of supernatural increase, secular education and employment in the world's system seem to be the only real choices to get ahead.

So when Ma and Pa are confronted with the projected financial costs of higher education, they are overwhelmed. Tuition, books, room and board, transportation, drugs, fraternity parties, condoms, alcohol, bail for civil disobedience rallies, abortions, four-dollar-a-bar "green" soap— these things add up! It is then that the state university becomes the only option. It is tax- subsidized, so the tuition is low. It is primarily run by godless heathens who have made themselves an enemy of God. It is "politically correct," so God or his people are not invited on campus.

It will have an extreme collectivist agenda to make sure the outdated philosophies of the founding fathers will never see the light of day in any classroom. Principles like national sovereignty, biblical morals, the God-given right of self-defense, no sex before marriage, telling the truth, the superiority of man over animals, sexual fidelity in marriage, free enterprise...all gone.

The history books will be conveniently revised to support the complete indoctrination process. Just read a few of the new "edited" editions. You'll come away thinking they're talking about a different country. I've got news for you, they are. The promotion of big government, big tax, and leftist, collectivist doctrine is imposed at every level of education.

But little Billy needs an education so he can get a job and make a living, so Mom and Dad send him off like a sheep led to the slaughter. Their lack of proper covenant training makes the new student an ideal candidate to have this young mind molded into another good secular humanist citizen. If he took any faith with him, the surrounding continuous assault will marginalize or completely defeat that small, flickering light. Without a sound basic foundation and strong support group, weak salt will not flavor its surroundings. Diluted faith can easily be worn down and become unfruitful.

JUST CORRECTING CHILDREN'S ERRORS IS NOT TRAINING!

Saying "Johnny, don't do that" is insufficient as a primary training tool. Merely telling children when they have done something wrong is not training. They must be educated and specifically trained in covenant principles. There must be impartation, a sowing into them.

This is a working spiritual principle. The mere apparent absence of flagrant, overt sin is not sufficient. You know—not doing the serious sins like robbing liquor stores, watching soap operas, buying lottery tickets, stealing cars, drinking whiskey, and sleeping with hookers. Call it the vacuum principle. If parents and the church don't fill that vacuum with truth, our culture and our children's untrained peers will fill it with deception and lies. If you don't sow truth, they will sow their version of it. There will be a crop, and there will be a harvest, and if you don't control the origin of the seed, you are going to get a harvest you really don't want to reap.

Other examples of the need to renew our minds include children having children, breeding versus true parenting, blind political party allegiance, repetitive non-fruit-bearing behavior, idle habits and useless wastes of time. There are so many packages of bad decisions based on false information leading to unwanted harvests.

The things you are involved with are a result of your decisions, good or bad. And those decisions will determine what, if any, spiritual power and influence will be available for you to arrive at your desired end. Focusing on God's agenda brings wisdom, the anointing of the Word of God, and the power of the Holy Spirit. Ungodly activities result in more deception, and you open yourself to more demonic influence. Remember, demons almost never travel alone—they bring some of their friends with them. Think about it. Is it any surprise that certain elected politicians who can't even figure out if they are a man or woman constantly make bad decisions on other issues of global importance?

CARNAL INFLUENCES

Let me help you with a few practical definitions:

Carnally minded means *governed by sense-realm input.* Carnally minded people's decisions are completely driven by avoiding personal, physical, or mental inconvenience. No victory is worth their discomfort.

Spiritually minded means *submitted to the Word of God, led by the Holy Spirit.* Spiritually minded people's decisions are not affected by personal inconvenience or cultural pressure.

Operating in true biblical faith is much easier on the mind when it has an abundance of Word to draw upon. The Word gives the Holy Spirit something to work with.

> *NOW FAITH is the assurance (the confirmation, the title deed) of the things [we] hope for, being the proof of things [we] do not see and the conviction of their reality [faith perceiving as real fact what is not revealed to the senses]. (Hebrews 11:1 AMP)*

> *Blessed is the man that walketh not in the counsel of the ungodly, nor standeth in the way of sinners, nor sitteth in the seat of the scornful. But his delight is in the law of the LORD; and in his law doth he meditate day and night. And he shall be like a tree planted by the rivers of water, that bringeth forth his fruit in his season; his leaf also shall not wither; and whatsoever he doeth shall prosper. (Psalm 1:1-3)*

> *The law of the LORD is perfect, converting the soul: the testimony of the LORD is sure, making wise the simple. (Psalm 19:7)*

> *And be not conformed to this world: but be ye transformed by the renewing of your mind, that ye may prove what is that good, and acceptable, and perfect, will of God. (Romans 12:2)*

> *Do not be conformed to this world (this age), [fashioned after and adapted to its external, superficial customs], but be transformed (changed) by the [entire] renewal of your mind [by its new ideals and its new attitude], so that you may prove [for yourselves] what*

is the good and acceptable and perfect will of God, even the thing which is good and acceptable and perfect [in His sight for you]. (Romans 12:2 AMP)

That ye put off concerning the former conversation the old man, which is corrupt according to the deceitful lusts; And be renewed in the spirit of your mind; And that ye put on the new man, which after God is created in righteousness and true holiness. (Ephesians 4:22-24)

Not by works of righteousness which we have done, but according to his mercy he saved us, by the washing of regeneration, and renewing of the Holy Spirit. (Titus 3:5)

Study to shew thyself approved unto God, a workman that needeth not to be ashamed, rightly dividing the word of truth. But shun profane and vain babblings: for they will increase unto more ungodliness. (II Timothy 2:15,16)

Study and be eager and do your utmost to present yourself to God approved (tested by trial), a workman who has no cause to be ashamed, correctly analyzing and accurately dividing [rightly handling and skillfully teaching] the Word of Truth. But avoid all empty (vain, useless, idle) talk, for it will lead people into more and more ungodliness. (II Timothy 2:15,16 AMP)

But if ye will not drive out the inhabitants of the land from before you; then it shall come to pass, that those which ye let remain of them shall be pricks in your eyes, and thorns in your sides, and shall vex you in the land wherein ye dwell. (Number 33:55)

When thou art come into the land which the LORD thy God giveth thee, thou shalt not learn to do after the abominations of those nations. (Deuteronomy 18:9)

Brethren, I count not myself to have apprehended: but this one thing I do, forgetting those things which are behind, and reaching forth unto those things which are before. (Philippians 3:13)

As obedient children, not fashioning yourselves according to the former lusts in your ignorance. (I Peter 1:14)

Let's look at Timothy again:

Study to shew thyself approved unto God, a workman that needeth not to be ashamed, rightly dividing the word of truth. (II Timothy 2:15,16)

If you do an in-depth word study of the word ashamed, you will find that word has several flavors. (Remember, words are containers. Like soup, the various ingredients produce the total flavor.) Webster's definition of the word ashamed includes *disappointed, delayed, confounded, confusion, become dry, put to confusion, bring reproach, disgraced, dishonor, unprepared, in a wrong position, out of position from whence action begins, out of place in relation to distribution.*

A broad-brush definition of ashamed means this: a person who is poorly trained and, due to laziness, has not put himself in a position to receive the blessings and favor of God when it was made available.

Remember the old computer adage, "Garbage in equals garbage out"? Why would we think it would be any different with our minds? Examples of sense-led, carnally minded behavior goes far beyond addictions to things like food, sex, and alcohol.

How do you react while waiting in line or when you're looking for a parking place? Here's the scene: There's a light rain coming down, and I'm on a grocery store parking lot in a nice neighborhood. The area is full of churches, and many people who live there profess to be Christians.

Stand back and watch out! Be careful! People are cutting in line, going the wrong way in parking lanes, cutting across lines of parked cars, and never even look for conflicting traffic. And forget about obeying the NO PARKING signs. And they don't care what color the curb is painted. Waiting traffic is lined up behind stubborn drivers who refuse to move until they get a closer spot to park. No matter what, they are not going to get wet! They don't care about being rude or how many traffic laws they break, they are just not going to get wet!

Later, as I'm coming out of the grocery store, there is a woman standing next to her teenage daughter with a cart full of groceries. She is literally hollering, "I'm wet! I'm wet!" Apparently, she attempted to make it to her car, and it rained on her. "Hey lady!" I want to yell, "It's only water! It's not battery acid!"

You see, a seemingly insignificant event, like getting wet, is a major issue for carnally minded people. And what was she teaching her child? She was passing on to her children more fears, more limits, more carnality, and more self-destructive behavior.

Speaking of teaching children, carnally minded people are constantly teaching their children, without even holding a formal class, and probably never realizing it. Here are a few lessons:

"Go get my cigarettes!"

"Get my beer so I don't have to get up off my fat butt and out of the recliner."

The child answers the telephone, and the parent says, "Tell them I'm not here."

A young family is riding along the highway on their way home from Bible study. The little boy asks his daddy, "What is that?" He's pointing to a small black box on the dash with the flashing red light and a wire coming out of it.

"Oh, that's Daddy's radar detector. That's what we use to deliberately break the law and try not to get caught."

Different scene, different magnitude, but is that any different than catching a would-be thief in somebody's backyard with a bag of burglar tools?

All scripture is given by inspiration of God, and is profitable for doctrine, for reproof, for correction, for instruction in righteousness: That the man of God may be perfect, thoroughly furnished unto all good works. (II Timothy 3:16,17)

Brother Fred Price taught us this many years ago. All scripture is truly stated. All scripture is not a statement of truth.

Examples:

And said, Naked came I out of my mother's womb, and naked shall I return thither: the LORD gave, and the LORD hath taken away; blessed be the name of the LORD. (Job 1:21)

The Lord taketh away? Job just didn't have the revelatory knowledge that Satan was the cause, not God. Based on some of the preaching I've heard, Job isn't the only one who got the answer to that question wrong.

And the serpent said unto the woman, Ye shall not surely die. (Genesis 3:4)

And Satan has been lying to the children of God ever since. Just so you can catch a few of those lies when they cross your path, I'll expose them here:

- Did God really say you could be healed?
- Do you really believe he'll give you your daily bread?
- Come on, you think you can pray-in your unsaved loved ones? You've got to be kidding.
- Do you think a loving God would allow someone to go to hell?

Lies! His purpose is to get you to doubt what God said so the devil can have your victory.

> *And be not drunk with wine, wherein is excess; but be filled with the Spirit; Speaking to yourselves in psalms and hymns and spiritual songs, singing and making melody in your heart to the Lord; Giving thanks always for all things unto God and the Father in the name of our Lord Jesus Christ; Submitting yourselves one to another in the fear of God. (Ephesians 5:18-21)*

Then there are so-called born-again Christians, filled with the Holy Spirit, the Anointer, who willingly agree to dull and confuse their senses with alcohol. Talk about cultural pressure.

> *That at that time ye were without Christ, being aliens from the commonwealth of Israel, and strangers from the covenants of promise, having no hope, and without God in the world: But now in Christ Jesus ye who sometimes were far off are made nigh by the blood of Christ. Now therefore ye are no more strangers and foreigners, but fellow citizens with the saints, and of the household of God. (Ephesians 2:12-13,19)*

> *That Christ may dwell in your hearts by faith; that ye, being rooted and grounded in love…(Ephesians 3:17)*

The carnal-minded believer who has not renewed his mind to the Word of God will be greatly limited in the fulfillment of his own personal spiritual destiny and will be of little use in building the kingdom of God.

The Soul (mind)
THE EGG CARTON *After Renewal*

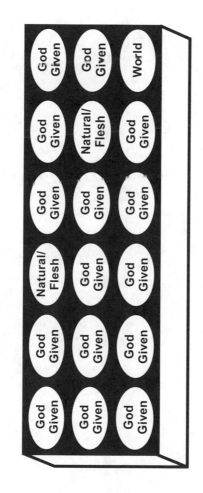

The soul (mind) is comprised of intellect, emotions, skills, habits, learned experiences, spiritual influences, training, inclinations, dispositions, morals, standards, fears, obsessions, priorities, memories, plans, and more.

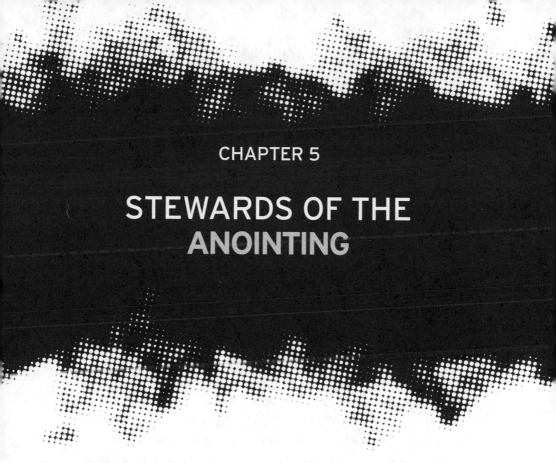

CHAPTER 5

STEWARDS OF THE ANOINTING

M erriam Webster's Collegiate Dictionary—Eleventh Edition defines stewardship as *the careful and responsible management of something entrusted to someone's care.*

It's amazing that God has entrusted something, *Someone,* so precious, so divine, so pure into the hands of his family. It can appear to be a daunting task, but God assures us that it is his way and within the capabilities he gives us. I picture it this way—every mind ought to have a bouncer at the door! We need a bouncer to guard our eye gate and ear gate.

Let's see what God's Word says about stewardship!

> *Let a man so account of us, as of the ministers of Christ [the Anointed One], and stewards [trustees] of the mysteries [the secret purposes] of God. (I Corinthians 4:1)*

> *And he said unto them, Take heed what ye hear. (Mark 4:24)*

Therefore if any man be in Christ, he is a new creature: old things are passed away; behold, all things are become new. (II Corinthians 5:17)

Now then we are ambassadors for Christ, as though God did beseech you by us: we pray you in Christ's stead, be ye reconciled to God. (II Corinthians 5:20)

We are Christ's ambassadors, appealing to people on his behalf, seeking to persuade them and bringing them into harmony with him.

So we are Christ's ambassadors, God making His appeal as it were through us. We [as Christ's personal representatives] beg you for His sake to lay hold of the divine favor [now offered you] and be reconciled to God. (II Corinthians 5:20 AMP)

Here is a special word to all you multicultural types. God didn't send me down here to learn all about how you do your religious stuff in your foreign land. I have no interest in your demon statues and funny masks or your weird outfits, chants, songs, amulets, and tokens.

Make no mistake about it, these objects that depict and glorify demonic entities are a point of contact with the spirit realm—the devil's spirits. Just stroll through one of the big import stores with your spiritual eyes open and see all of the demonically inspired stuff being bought by oblivious American consumers and taken back to their homes to be proudly put on display. These things display a level of evil and spiritual ignorance that should not be found in the home of a believer.

Don't give me the speech that we're not under the law anymore. Just look in Leviticus to see how God really feels about these symbols and what he told the high priest to do about it.

As I travel around the world, I naturally observe how people from other cultures dress and how they season their food. I might even try some of their cuisine and enjoy it. I'm OK with some of the colorful artwork or maybe some games or amusements or dinner choices. But don't hand me any of your demonic spiritual mumbo jumbo. I don't care about all your counterfeit gods. They're all dead anyway. I don't want your tokens, charms, amulets, or symbols. I don't care about all of the folklore of your so-called spirit life. If Jesus isn't the center of it, it's all devil worship anyway. My job is to tell you about the one and true God and his plan for all mankind.

I'm reminded of an incident at a dinner party where I was making casual conversation with a couple of the other guests. My precious wife was there with me, encouraging me to be on my best behavior and not start anything.

Right in the middle of the conversation, up comes the topic of teaching religion to children. I didn't start it, I didn't bring it up, it wasn't my fault, you see, but you probably have noticed by now that demons recognize the power and anointing of the Holy Spirit in a believer, and occasionally they will manifest themselves.

So here is this secular, carnal couple, educated far beyond their intellect, beginning to present their lofty opinion concerning religious training for their two daughters. The mother says, "I am just going to raise them to be neutral. Then they can make up their own minds when they're older."

Well, up from my belly jumps this loud voice that says, "Oh! So you're going to raise them to be devil worshipers!" The woman looks at me like I'm from another planet.

It is difficult for me to be silent in the face of such spiritual ignorance. If you do not sow the truth, deception is the default setting. A word to you parents—someone will sow something into your children. If it's not you or the men and women of God sowing truth, it will be the devil's crowd sowing lies and deception, and the manifestation (fruit) of the curse will be available for all to see.

> And all thy children shall be taught of the LORD; and great shall be the peace of thy children. In righteousness shalt thou be established: thou shalt be far from oppression; for thou shalt not fear: and from terror; for it shall not come near thee. (Isaiah 54:13,14)

And all thy children shall be taught of the Lord, and great shall be the peace of thy children (wholeness, completeness, nothing missing, nothing broken). You will be established in righteousness. What a description of victory!

Now please keep in mind that young people would be included in that description of children, but not to the exclusion of all the children of God. Each of us at any age should be taught the truth of the covenants of God. The anointing which resides on the Word of God should mark our lives, changing us for his glory, preparing us to be used by God for kingdom-building by using covenant principles.

Just imagine a giant scale like the scales of justice down at the courthouse weighing all the evidence of a case. In your life, most of the evidence presented for your consideration has come from the culture and not the covenant. Our job as believers is to change that abundance in our minds and in our spirit man.

All of those useless, non-fruit-bearing, demonically inspired pieces of error-filled information that have built up over the years need to be replaced. This is what Jesus was speaking about when he said to guard what goes in your ears and in front of your eyes. The good news is you are in charge of your abundance.

Is it any wonder that if your abundance is full of the culture you will have problems producing covenant results? You're in charge of the scale. You see the results Isaiah promised if you are taught of the Lord. Paul tries to get it through our thick heads in the 12th chapter of Romans:

> *And be not conformed to this world: but be ye transformed by the renewing of your mind, that ye may prove what is that good, and acceptable, and perfect, will of God. (Romans 12:2)*

> *Do not be conformed to this world (this age), [fashioned after and adapted to its external, superficial customs], but be transformed (changed) by the [entire] renewal of your mind [by its new ideals and its new attitude], so that you may prove [for yourselves] what is the good and acceptable and perfect will of God, even the thing*

which is good and acceptable and perfect [in His sight for you].
(Romans 12:2 AMP)

So you can prove the word out for yourself. This is what the renewing-of-your-mind process is all about—changing the evidence in your abundance for your spirit man to consider, present to your mind, then make a decision and act.

In a recent survey, high school graduates were asked about various people and topics. When asked about popular sports figures, most of the boys were able to list dozens of team names, players, and game statistics. The young girls were equally skilled in naming popular music stars, fashion designers, make-up manufacturers, and the like.

Less than forty percent could name the Vice President of the United States. Less than twenty percent could name the Chief Justice of the Supreme Court, and only a small number could give the names of their elected representatives or senators. The numbers were equally dismal concerning their rights as citizens described in the U.S. Constitution.

It's clear that they have been trained by the culture and not by the covenant. Are you still surprised about the outcome of this current experiment in self-government? Now since this was a secular public school survey, it wasn't exactly a quiz on the book of Proverbs. Can you imagine the outcome of that? Could I ask you parents about YOUR kids? Oh, oh, there he goes again getting into your business. Why are these personal challenges inappropriate? True Christian parenting is a far more serious matter than merely breeding offspring with the same last name.

You will be diligent about letting something in your eye gate and ear gate and putting that into your abundance. The question is, what will you be diligent about? What kind of information will your mind focus on? How easily people are grossly misled in today's economy or political arena, simply due to their ignorance of truth and blind reliance on tradition and rumor.

TRAINED BY THE CULTURE
vs. TRAINED BY THE COVENANT

Where are you getting your information?

The choice is yours!

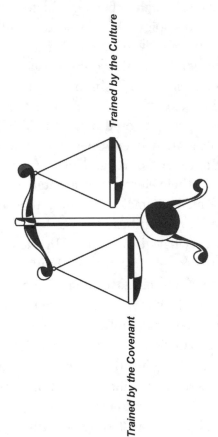

Trained by the Culture

Trained by the Covenant

Refuse to be Unteachable

How sad it is that this applies to the church. We are participating members of the most fantastic supernatural organization on earth, yet we are mostly oblivious to the bylaws and membership benefits.

If you are not operating in the anointing, you revert back to natural, charitable works and end up doing good, moral acts, mostly alms deeds, which do not require the anointing. There's nothing wrong with alms deeds. My wife is my agreement partner in these matters, and we have set aside a fixed percentage of our total income for alms giving. We feel this is a real application of covenant principle.

If I have twenty dollars and I buy a bag of groceries and deliver it to the widow when she is having financial lack, it's a good work. But that good deed really doesn't require the supernatural burden-removing, yoke-destroying power of God. *But consider doing those works which require the anointing.*

What if I went to her and sowed the word of faith concerning seed time and harvest? What if she began to walk in revelatory knowledge and responded by planting a seed for abundance and took a stand of faith for manifestation? You may wish to study the anointing of increase in my upcoming book, *The Believer's Financial Workshop.* When our faith couples with the anointing, we're truly doing business for God.

Remember, spiritual gifts don't make you grow; time in the Word and proving it out in your life does that.

LIMITATIONS ON THE ANOINTING

In case you haven't noticed, there are many situations where the anointing doesn't seem to work like it is supposed to. Limitations on the anointing include doubt and unbelief.

> *And he did not many mighty works there because of their unbelief. (Matthew 13:58)*

And he could there do no mighty work, save that he laid his hands upon a few sick folk, and healed them. And he marveled because of their unbelief. And he went round about the villages, teaching (Mark 6:5,6)

Did you catch that? What did Jesus do when even his personal anointing couldn't produce the desired results? He went around *teaching the Word of God*!

THE LIMITATION OF TRADITION

Howbeit in vain do they worship me, teaching for doctrines the commandments of men. For laying aside the commandment of God, ye hold the tradition of men, as the washing of pots and cups: and many other such like things ye do. And he said unto them, Full well ye reject the commandment of God, that ye may keep your own tradition. (Mark 7:7-9)

Thus have ye made the commandment of God of none effect by your tradition. Ye hypocrites, well did Esaias prophesy of you, saying, This people draweth nigh unto me with their mouth, and honoureth me with their lips; but their heart is far from me. But in vain they do worship me, teaching for doctrines the commandments of men. And he called the multitude, and said unto them, Hear, and understand: Not that which goeth into the mouth defileth a man; but that which cometh out of the mouth, this defileth a man. (Matthew 15:6-11)

LACK OF FAITH

And it came to pass on a certain day, as he was teaching, that there were Pharisees and doctors of the law sitting by, which were come out of every town of Galilee, and Judaea, and Jerusalem: and the power of the Lord was present to heal them. (Luke 5:17)

The Anointed One was present with the power to heal. None of those religious leaders received anything; just the guy who got lowered down through the roof got what he came for. Faith and the anointing joined up to produce the results.

STRIFE

One of the meanings of the word strife is an evil undercurrent. The mere presence of strife hinders the power of God (the anointing) from flowing through us. It has a negative effect on pure worship. Strife distorts our attitude toward receiving a manifestation of a promise from God. Strife harbors bitterness and resentful feelings. It leads to offense, and offense will stop the flow of the anointing resulting in selfishness, fear, and resentment. Peter instructed us that it hinders our prayers from being answered. Agreement promotes the flow of the anointing.

> *Flee also youthful lusts: but follow righteousness, faith, charity, peace, with them that call on the Lord out of a pure heart. (II Timothy 2:22)*

> *Shun youthful lusts and flee from them, and aim at and pursue righteousness (all that is virtuous and good, right living, conformity to the will of God in thought, word, and deed); [and aim at and pursue] faith, love, [and] peace (harmony and concord with others) in fellowship with all [Christians], who call upon the Lord out of a pure heart. (II Timothy 2:22 AMP)*

You must decide to rule your tongue. You must decide to not tolerate strife. Loose the anointing of truth, honesty, and peace to conquer strife. Expect our loving God to bring you into harmony and grant you total victory over strife.

Many years ago as I was teaching a study class on faith, a student presented a challenge she was going through. The lady was a public school teacher and her class was in chaos. The small children simply were out of control, restless, noisy, and apparently immune to discipline. Actual learning was nearly non-existent in this environment.

Now I'll bet each one of you mother-types has her own bag of suggestions. The options are many. Yelling with a loud voice to restore order (as if order ever existed), physical restraints like duct tape or rope, or an appeal to their parents (I can hear some of you laughing). Do you really think the little darlings behave any better at home?

Here was our solution: The school teacher, the students in my class, and I took the proper spiritual authority over the enemy and looked to God for a plan. Since we were studying faith and the anointing, loosing the burden-removing, yoke-destroying power of God, this seemed like an appropriate course of action. After we prayed about it, it seemed good to us and the Holy Spirit to use anointed prayer cloths.

> *And God wrought special miracles by the hands of Paul: So that from his body were brought unto the sick handkerchiefs or aprons, and the diseases departed from them, and the evil spirits went out of them. (Acts 19:11,12)*

Our teacher took small sections of cloth, which we had prayed over, and placed them out of view on the bottoms of each of the children's chairs. With the full confidence of an accomplished faith warrior, she expected godly results. Any guess what happened? The peaceful transformation was amazing. The power and presence of God had created a peaceful atmosphere conducive to the goal—teaching the children. Praise God for another victory.

Since that incident, many people have experienced similar results flowing from the anointing—some even without knowing the source. Try it sometime at your house or work place where strife has made its attack.

I have often told my classes that I have great confidence in their abilities as they learn to flow in the anointing. My statement goes something like this: I believe that you could take a believer, one well-accomplished in the word of faith, well-skilled in the anointing, and parachute him or her into a foreign country. There he could take the place of any advisor or cabinet member of the national government and provide superior, accurate, and useful, godly counsel to the head of state. An outrageous claim? Go to Isaiah Chapter 11:

> And the spirit of the LORD shall rest upon him, the spirit of wisdom and understanding, the spirit of counsel and might, the spirit of knowledge and of the fear of the LORD. (Isaiah 11:2)

In verse two we read that the spirit of the Lord shall rest upon him, the spirit of wisdom and understanding, the spirit of counsel (*sound advice*) and might (*supernatural empowerment*), the spirit of knowledge, and the fear of the Lord. If that's what Isaiah expected to happen to Jesus, the flesh-and-blood man from Nazareth, and if I am in Christ (the Anointed One and his anointing), and if Christ (the Anointed One and his anointing) is in me, why should I expect any different results in me or in you?

Let's be real. *Who* do you want making the critical decisions here on earth—decisions about war, peace, distribution of wealth, justice, mercy, dominion, development, truth, and abundance? An unregenerated secular heathen, trained by a demonically inspired culture who has rejected God and places no value on the Word of God? Or a covenant-trained believer, submitted to the Word of God, led by the Holy Spirit, and inspired by LOVE Himself?

Remember, one of the flavors of the word ecclesiastic is *governance.*

Let me give you an additional example of practical anointing: for a period of time in my life, I was an estimator for a construction company. This was somewhat ironic as I had never worked in the construction industry nor had any formal training in construction practices and techniques. But my working there was the will of God because of the spiritual relationship I share with the owners of the company. We all had to trust in the anointing that God had placed on me to do the right thing and to learn the technical skills necessary to do my job correctly.

One day, I arrived at a job site and found three various construction crews engaged in a confusing discussion. There were framers, specialty carpenters, and various subcontractors all gathered around a set of construction plans trying to figure out what went where and who was to do what job next without getting into each others' way. These are skilled workmen, their experience and knowledge far exceeding anything I had to offer in the natural realm.

Those of you who are in business will immediately recognize the seriousness of this problem. Here were ten or twelve highly paid, highly specialized workers who were "dead in the water" and accomplishing nothing. Time and payroll money were being wasted. Something had to happen and happen now. They needed leadership, some insight into the situation, some plan which would make the project work out.

After asking a few questions to properly define the problem, I withdrew to a quiet spot under a tree on the far side of the lot. I explained to God what he obviously already knew—I was in over my head, and nothing in my background or education was going to provide sufficient information and knowledge to solve the problem.

But wait a minute! I am a believer, a little anointed one, part of the church of the living God, empowered by the Holy Spirit, and not dependant on operating exclusively on natural, intellectual resources. The Anointed One is within me. After acknowledging his presence and requesting that timely help of the personal ministry of the Holy Spirit, three things, seemingly unrelated, came to mind.

Not fully comprehending how these facts might apply to the circumstances, I returned to the discussion and voiced the three things. Now keep in mind that I didn't know if there was another person at this construction site who knew anything about God or his anointing. But I know him and his anointed.

You may be the only person at your job or in your family who is relying on the supernatural intervention of God. You may be his only conduit at that point in time to distribute the anointing.

Well, you probably know the end of the story. The various parties to the discussion immediately recognized the accurate wisdom of my (his) observations. It was as if the key pieces of a puzzle were suddenly discovered. The groups went on about their tasks, and production resumed. Now here was a good place for me not to get my ego inflated about being a distributor of supernatural knowledge, wisdom, and understanding. I know I'm not that smart. *It is not me that doeth the works, but my father in me.* That's what the scripture says.

EXAMPLES OF PRACTICAL ANOINTING

I was at the estate attorney's office as he was preparing the instruments of transfer for the family real estate to the heirs. A major oversight by the preparing attorney failed to include a debt-free transfer of the real property to the son-in-law in the event of the preceding death of the daughter. If not corrected in the documents, this could have resulted in significant debt and certain tax consequences.

While I was reviewing the draft documents, the Holy Spirit pointed out the omission to me and I showed it to counsel. The problem was easily corrected before the documents were all executed by the parties. Score another one of life's victories for the Holy Spirit.

Remember the fellows who didn't know about the Holy Spirit?

> *And it came to pass, that, while Apollos was at Corinth, Paul having passed through the upper coasts came to Ephesus: and finding certain disciples, He said unto them, Have ye received the Holy Spirit since ye believed? And they said unto him, We have not so much as heard whether there be any Holy Spirit. And he said unto them, Unto what then were ye baptized? And they*

said, Unto John's baptism. Then said Paul, John verily baptized with the baptism of repentance, saying unto the people, that they should believe on him which should come after him, that is, on Christ [the Anointed One] Jesus. When they heard this, they were baptized in the name of the Lord Jesus. And when Paul had laid his hands upon them, the Holy Spirit came on them; and they spake with tongues, and prophesied. (Acts 19:1-6)

And a certain Jew named Apollos, born at Alexandria, an eloquent man, and mighty in the scriptures, came to Ephesus. This man was instructed in the way of the Lord; and being fervent in the spirit, he spake and taught diligently the things of the Lord, knowing only the baptism of John. And he began to speak boldly in the synagogue: whom when Aquila and Priscilla had heard, they took him unto them, and expounded unto him the way of God more perfectly. (Acts 18:24-26)

For with great power he refuted the Jews in public [discussions], showing and proving by the Scriptures that Jesus is the Christ (the Messiah) (The anointed One). (Acts 18:28 AMP)

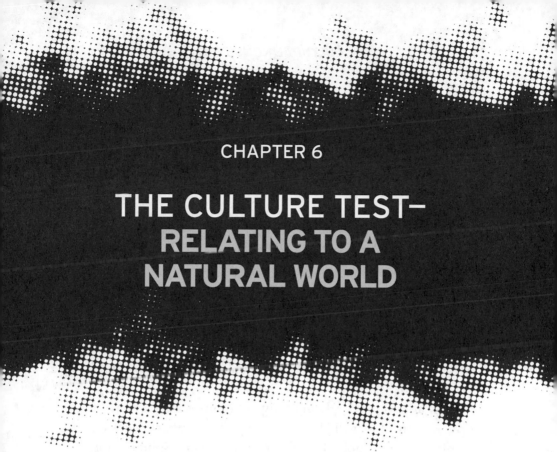

CHAPTER 6

THE CULTURE TEST– RELATING TO A NATURAL WORLD

M any Christians have difficulty relating to biblical healing for their bodies or increase in their finances because they don't really understand the proper relationship between the believer, God, and the natural realm.

Why would God need a natural realm anyway? Our God is a spirit being. Without a natural body, most of the demands and things needed for life down here in this material world are unnecessary. Think about it. What good are the material things of this world to an infinite spirit being? Yet he has given us all things which pertain to life and godliness.

According as his divine power hath given unto us all things that pertain unto life and godliness. (II Peter 1:3)

By the way, he created all these things by speaking his word in faith. We are made in the likeness of his image, and that's what we are empowered to do—to create our own universe, if you will. But that is another lesson in the basics of Faith School. I hope you're using that impartation and the power of your tongue to frame your world with powerful, faith-inspired words of covenant and our promised abundant life.

> *Death and life are in the power of the tongue: and they that love*
> *it shall eat the fruit thereof. (Proverbs 18:21)*

Try this view: The natural, material world is the stage—the arena where God uses the believer to display his eternal, supernatural principles, and where his truths are demonstrated, proven, and verified for all to see (except, perhaps, those who are completely blind spiritually).

Look at it this way: If the only Bible promise you have going for you in this life is the heaven thing after you die, you are going to this place that nobody has ever seen. Every Sunday morning, two hundred thousand preachers are all talking about heaven, and none of them has ever been there. If the heaven thing is IT for you, you won't know if the preacher told you the truth until it's too late to change your mind.

On the other hand, if you search the scriptures and find a covenant benefit or promise you are entitled to as a believer, one which has yet to manifest in your life, you have the high privilege of taking a stand of faith. With patience, you can see it through to completion and receive it down here in the natural. When that promise becomes a reality in this earthly realm, that's biblical manifestation, and that's what real faith is all about.

If you understand the proper relationship between us and the natural, material world, you'll be able to understand the importance of covenant giving. If God is love, our actions should reflect the one who created us and instructs us on how to behave. Love gives. Giving is the mainstay of Christian life. Giving plays a prominent role in all of our thinking, speaking, and acting. Look how easily that fits into the natural realm.

While the earth remaineth, seedtime and harvest. (Gen. 8:22)

Giving is like planting seeds. A loving, kind word of instruction to a child is a seed planted toward a harvest of a caring, considerate adult. A strong, unchanging word of correction to a child is a seed planted toward a harvest of a self-disciplined, obedient adult. A decision of truth and honor when faced with a temptation to steal is a seed of the force of righteousness planted towards a harvest of character, integrity, and order in the world.

A teaching and demonstration of a covenant Bible principle is a seed planted toward a harvest of a peaceful and joyous long life in a family. The faithful, godly labors of a pastor to his flock are a seed planted towards a harvest of stability, success, and community service in that neighborhood.

A vote cast and a campaign contribution made for an honorable candidate who is a believer and follows godly principles is a seed planted towards a harvest of peace, justice, and prosperity in our nation. (Remember, God's biblical plan for us is self-government and free moral choice.)

The daily, dedicated efforts of a Christian businessman to serve his customers quality goods and services is a seed planted towards a harvest of a Book-of-Proverbs-style morality in the marketplace. Paying off someone else's car loan, credit card balances, or house mortgage is a seed planted towards a harvest of the biblical debt-free lifestyle.

Helping out a single mother and her children after her no-good husband has taken off by paying her rent three months in advance, getting her a solid vehicle to drive, putting some groceries on the table and on the shelves, taking care of the electric bill, giving her money for gas and care for the kids are all seeds of God's love planted towards a harvest of blessing and provision.

Giving alms gifts to the poor and needy, those who seem unable to provide for themselves, are seeds planted towards a harvest of obedience to God's Word, which says to focus on blessing others and not receiving for ourselves. The receiving comes as part of the principle.

The major capital investment in a Christian businessman's plant, machinery, equipment, and staff training are seeds planted towards a harvest of well-paying jobs for the employees, company benefits for the workers, a stable, harmonious place for the team to labor and produce goods and services for others.

The sacrificial offering from a believer fulfilling his ministry role as a giver, sending a costly financial gift offering to the man or woman of God to help build God's kingdom here on earth, is a seed planted towards a harvest of souls, a harvest of biblical morality and Christian dominion, a harvest of true biblical increase. (See Second Corinthians 9 AMP.)

The very principle that rules the laws and sciences of this earth, seedtime and harvest, is a reflection of the love of God, and he uses the believer down here in the natural realm to display it. It is there for the unbeliever to see. You can demonstrate it, and show the goodness of God's heart.

> *He did this that He might clearly demonstrate through the ages to come the immeasurable (limitless, surpassing) riches of His free grace (His unmerited favor) in [His] kindness and goodness of heart toward us in Christ Jesus. (Ephesians 2:7 AMP)*

So what about all the cheeseburgers, designer clothes, expensive cars and all that other stuff?

Let's take a little quiz to see how you're coming along in relating to a natural world. This is going to be pretty simple; just make one of the two choices. (Here's a little spiritual hint: If you are *really* having a problem deciding between these two answers, that's an indication of the need for more Bible-based training in the area of biblical wealth, stewardship, and abundance.)

God's divine purpose for cheeseburgers is:

A. For flesh-driven, carnal-minded human beings to eat without limit or regard for self-control.
B. Just one of the many major food groups available down here in the natural realm. (Come on…lighten up.)

God's divine purpose for clothes is:

A. To create a multibillion-dollar fashion industry of styles which go in and out of favor on a regular basis. To force buyers who have no core values and simply exist on peer group recognition and approval of others to become slaves to a never-ending cycle of mindless expensive buying, displaying on their bodies (for a short time), and then throwing away multiple closets full of over-priced, useless, imported junk. Key word in your vocabulary might be "cool" or "hot" (neither one actually referring to the outside temperature), or whatever the "in" phrase of the day is.
B. A basic tool of life, to keep cool or warm or dry, protect the body from the elements of the earth, as an outer layer to stay clean when working, not get burned when welding, and what seems to be needed in the present culture. Above all, to cover up that body of yours and present yourself in every social situation as modest, decent, virtuous and proper. (If I see one more belly button on a preteen girl wearing some revealing little nothing that looks like her PARENTS bought it for her from a hooker's supply catalog…don't get me started.)

(The quiz continues below. Allow me this small rabbit trail please!)

So I walk into my Sunday morning class to begin teaching the students. A fashionably dressed young woman walks in, and my attention is immediately drawn to her new dress shoes. From the front, the shoes appear to be perfectly sensible, useful shoes. But when she turns and walks away towards her seat, a design flaw becomes apparent. The shoes have no backs! The fronts have laces and a knot which serves no function whatsoever (fake, useless). The backs are completely open. The design offers no way to secure the shoe to her foot, just an effortless way to kick the shoes off.

Think about that for a second. The shoe couldn't actually perform its intended task (to secure, protect, equip). But it was easy to take off. Its only possible attribute was style. Does this situation have a parallel truth? Now this particular design of shoe might be useful for inside the house to wear like slippers, just like rubber flip-flops might be perfect for walking the beach or showering at the gym. But for walking outside, appearing socially in public, or in a situation where one might be expected to perform a task such as run, jump, climb a ladder, walk a long distance, unload the truck, stack boxes, chase children, push a stalled car?

Let's get real. Many people have selected their everyday personal fashion statement to be "poor people coming back from the beach." Tee-shirts as outerwear? Pants with no belt or pockets? Shoes with no backs? The woman in cold weather, wearing a heavy jacket and flip flops? These choices make a statement, and the statement is clear and simple. That person's only priority is following some current fad or personal convenience with no interest in being prepared for the practicalities of life. If an emergency or even everyday chores required action...well, you get the idea.

(Okay, back to the quiz!)

God's divine purpose for a vehicle is:

A. An extravagant display of self-centered personal preferences, which reveal internal insecurities that are comforted by the selection and share-cropper ownership with the lender of some "thing" which assures us our rightful place with the cultural "in" crowd. This, along with the fact that the mere ownership of such a vehicle is so far beyond the person's financial reach that even the bank lets the tenant take seven years to pay off the bank's profitable financial interest in the transaction, all while the depreciating value of this asset is sinking faster than the Titanic. The owner-operator's level of knowledge of this complex machine likely is at a failing-grade status, so he is subject to a series of expensive repairs that place him at the mercy of a sharply trained salesman and shop service writer, both skilled in commission sales and the ability to remove large amounts of money from the checkbook of the hapless owner/operator/driver/payment-maker.

B. A well-chosen, affordable, dependable, well-maintained, presentable, safe vehicle in which its total ownership, operation, overall condition, state of maintenance, cleanliness, and regular availability all reflect a useful tool in meeting the needs and successfully completing the necessary transportation chores of life down here in this three-dimensional world. (Wow!)

God's divine purpose for transport planes and ocean-going freighters is:

A. For the daily delivery of countless containers and pallets stocked with every conceivable near-useless item to feed an economic engine of advertising-image-driven, mind-numbed consumers whose purchases are easily swayed by the color of the packaging, the mere appearance of the words "new and improved" or "imported," and equipped with such poor consumer skills they are unable to determine the practical application and use of most products unless the product appeals to the most base and primitive urges of the new owner.

B. Transportation as a means of conveyance, an important part in the chain of delivery of raw materials and quality finished goods, a valuable tool in ethical commerce and God's biblical system of free enterprise to provide common-sense merchandise options to an informed and well-supplied public, as an instantly available carrier to dispatch food, shelter, medical facilities, and everyday supplies to people in need around the world in times of famine, storms, poverty, and after the failure of demonically inspired economic systems (alms deeds).

Take, for example, a current fad and one of my personal pet peeves: stink candles. (Uh-oh...here we go!) Imported from a far-off land (it seems like everything comes from China these days), scented with rare oils and flavors to give your house, your business office, or car that sweet, sickening smell of rancid composting flowers.

Give me a break. Don't even try to tell me these things smell like real flowers or fresh herbs. They are just another cheap counterfeit of the real thing that some people will accept instead of the genuine article. You can fill your own personal environment with that fake stench if you want to, but let me help shed some light on the real issue. In case you didn't realize this, these fake fragrances are specifically designed to cover up unwanted odors more than they are meant to add something real or genuine.

And where do these sources of foul, rotten odors originate? They come from unclean houses and offices and cars. These are products deliberately designed, manufactured, distributed and sold to alleviate the guilt of poor stewardship. So don't hand me some song and dance—clean the house! Vacuum the car and get the carpets cleaned! Disinfect that bathroom for a change instead of trying to cover up the stench!

The following is a "Beverly-approved" story. (God gave me my precious wife to help keep me civilized and socially acceptable.)

We had been invited to a woman's house for dinner, and as soon as we walked into the entryway that foul odor of scented, rotting weeds smacked me right in the face. There on the table before me was a big bowl of that awful stuff (you may know it as potpourri). The smell was nearly overwhelming. I knew that the pleasing aromas of whatever carefully prepared foods we were about to be served would be completely overshadowed by this fake, rancid, chemical smell. So I made a command decision. (Please use this as a learning experience, not as a personal behavior example.)

At that moment, the effect this terrible product would have on our visit far outweighed my respect for personal property rights. As the lady disappeared back around the corner into her kitchen, I moved in on the offending bowl with all the stealth of a trained undercover agent, hid it behind my back, quickly stepped outside and dumped it into the garden behind the shrubs, exactly where the substance belonged anyway. My mission completed, I sat down to enjoy an otherwise pleasant, stink-free visit.

On the way home, I completed the obligatory admission of sin and Christian repentance, which included a confession to my wife of the deed that I had done. I received an appropriate teaching on the importance of "being nice." Another lesson to civilize me.

Now the demands of the marketplace have progressed to a point where bowls of the evil substance are not enough. Companies must produce small electrical stink appliances, which, when plugged into the nearest household electrical outlet, continuously emit a fowl odorous gas, available in a wide variety of dreadful false flavors, to cover up the resultant smells of one's non-cleaning.

And that leads me to another topic (I'm not done yet): floor carpeting. Having spent many years in the construction and remodeling industry, I have had the opportunity to observe the human species in their native habitat, the family home. The original purpose of floor carpeting has long ago passed from consideration for most home-owner-operators. Its sole function now is to provide a convenient, effortless place to store and hide the family filth and not have to clean up after themselves.

Watch the process of floor carpet replacement at one of your neighbor's houses. Pay particular attention to the removal of that mysterious brown layer of "fabric" down there. The buildup of crud is amazing: hair, scabs, pet debris, onion peelings, baby vomit...well, you get the point. The potential for contagious-disease transfer is astronomical. I'm surprised the E.P.A. doesn't make carpet installers wear those protective outfits you see in the science fiction plague movies. Think about that the next time you visit lazy Aunt Mary and you let little Billy get down on the floor to play. He should be sprayed with disinfectant as soon as you leave.

Of course, I'm sure none of *your* carpets are like that.

So, Brother David, you mean true stewardship over the natural realm would include having a high-quality vacuum cleaner, using it regularly, and then having the floor carpeting professionally sanitized on a frequent basis? Now you're getting to that proper relationship between the believer and the natural, material world.

I'll show you another personal reality indicator in the home: plastic flowers. If your house has a collection of plastic flowers, there is a spiritual yellow caution light flashing all over the place. Why? Because down here in the natural, you are willing to take the easy way out to accept the false—a substitute or counterfeit—something which provides none of the true qualities of the genuine, but just a hollow, pale image of the real flower, but with less effort and investment required.

Are you one of the countless believers who is content to accept the fake because it is easier and doesn't cost as much? What's the next compromise for you? Mashed potatoes out of a box? Vegetables out of a can? Bible study out of a fifteen-minute-per-week quarterly? Fictional DVDs, movies, and fables instead of a real life? Letting others do all of your Bible study for you? Watching a cable TV show about a beautiful place instead of actually going there because it's too much trouble?

God's divine purpose for the medical community is:

    A.   Develop a price-gouging, unworkable system that limits your medical options and obscenely profits from your physical frailty and makes you become dependent on pharmaceuticals and pay huge portions of your after-tax discretionary income to drain away large percentages of your wealth so it is nearly impossible to properly fund the building of the kingdom of God and fund the end-time harvest of souls. (Debt and medical expenses are the two biggest ways the enemy uses to siphon off the wealth of the believer and to divert the money from its real intended task of Kingdom-building.)

    B.   Provide a short-term medical fix to believers while they are learning to flow in the healing anointing that is operating in their lives, removing every burden and destroying every yoke. To keep people alive who are outside of the family of God till they get saved and healed.

God's divine purpose for television, internet, communication satellites, telephones, radio stations, printing, and publication businesses is:

A. To create an information delivery system for Satan to continuously bombard the eyes, ears, and senses of humans with demonically inspired ideas and concepts and images which are in conflict with biblical principles and to further distract believers from their primary direction of obeying God by getting them to focus on superficial entertainment and amusements, which leads to time-wasting and no fruit production.

B. A wonderful high-tech telecommunications, audio-visual-information data network to train, bless, educate, declare, and distribute the truths of God. A means by which we can easily stay in touch with other believers all over the world and share testimonies of victory and stories of love. In terms of news, a conduit of communication to point out sin and demonic activity to be dealt with immediately at the hands of covenant believers. To provide entertainment which inspires and motivates us to a higher level of godly morality.

God's divine purpose for hotels, stadiums, conference centers, meeting halls, and resorts is:

A. Provide a gathering place for heathens and believers alike, to blend together and be influenced by those whose father is the devil. In some cases, these buildings are financed by generations of unaware taxpayers who are blindly entertained by a series of distracting events held at the facility—people who fail to focus on the burden of debt being passed on to their grandchildren by government.

B.   Provide gathering places where God and godly principles are lifted up, where heathen are invited to attend, to hear the Word, become saved, set free, trained, and turned loose into the world as Kingdom builders.

Are you getting it now? God doesn't need the natural realm just for him. The natural realm is a place where he can reveal himself to us. And when you become skilled in the covenant, you will be able to reach into that unseen, supernatural realm on purpose, and with faith and patience pull out those things you have need of, and they will manifest into this natural, material world, into your life. That's the high privilege of the born-again, Spirit-filled, Bible-believing, covenant-trained believer.

The natural world was God's idea, and his creation is his thought, not mine. I'm glad he left me the manual on how to run things for him while I'm down here. So since it's his system, does God owe me a living? Do I have a biblical right to a cheeseburger?

The young lions lack food and suffer hunger, but they who seek (inquire of and require) the Lord [by right of their need and on the authority of His Word], none of them shall lack any beneficial thing. (Psalm 34:10 AMP)

Did you ever hear someone say this? "I didn't ask to be born." Usually when you hear that phrase, someone is bitterly complaining about his lot in life. To me, it is merely a true statement of fact. The arrangement of my birth was not a personal, conscious decision on my part. I didn't ask to be born. That's not a complaint.

So if this earth-thing was God's idea, and the fact that I need to live in a natural, physical body was God's idea, then this eating, bathing, going to the bathroom cycle is all part of his plan. And if we are his children, does he not have a covenant obligation to provide for us? Don't you have a covenant obligation to provide for your natural children?

Can you see how that takes the pressure off? Faithfully receiving our daily bread is just part of the plan. The Gentile heathens should be the only ones who are uptight about getting "the stuff."

> *Wherefore, if God so clothe the grass of the field, which today is, and tomorrow is cast into the oven, shall he not much more clothe you, O ye of little faith? Therefore take no thought, saying, What shall we eat? or, What shall we drink? or, Wherewithal shall we be clothed? (For after all these things do the Gentiles seek:) for your heavenly Father knoweth that ye have need of all these things. (Matthew 6:30-32)*

When you accept your true position as God's anointed instrument to exercise dominion over the earth and demonstrate his covenant, you start to see a proper relationship between you as a believer and the natural, physical realm. Your "stuff" has meaning. Everything you have has a testimony—when it was obtained by faith!

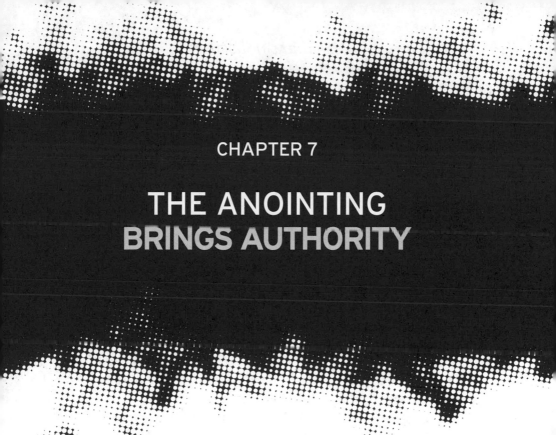

CHAPTER 7

THE ANOINTING
BRINGS AUTHORITY

J esus appointed seventy people to go out and declare the Gospel. He sent forth these laborers into the harvest giving them specific instructions, directions, and a code of conduct. Upon their return they rejoiced saying, "Even the devils are subject to us through thy name."

And the seventy returned again with joy, saying, Lord, even the devils are subject unto us through thy name. (Luke 10:17)

We can't pass over this without observing the establishment of a chain of command, which includes the authority of the believer to cast out devils. The use of the name of Jesus is one of the ways which the Anointed One empowers us believers to loose the burden-removing and yoke-destroying power of God into the earth. Their joy and amazement was present even when they obviously had just conducted a series of deliverance meetings.

Frankly, their response seems a little different than some modern-day church elders I have seen in similar circumstances.

I had just finished my ninety-minute teaching class and was comfortably resting in the pew listening to the pastor one Sunday morning. A couple of the church elders approached me and motioned for me to come with them. Out in the hallway, they explained that they had a problem case in the deliverance room.

As I arrive, I see a beautiful young woman, maybe mid-twenties, stunningly dressed and sitting in a metal chair in the middle of the room. There are a couple of dear, sweet grandmother-types patting her on the hand and telling her, "Jesus loves you." The woman responds by speaking unintelligibly in a low, soft voice, and when the elder lady leans in to hear, the young woman lashes out and tries to bite her. The other lady pats her on the hand and tells her everything is going to be all right. Obviously, there is no progress being made in setting this woman free.

As I approach, I aim my old Kings James Bible right at her. The well-meaning but spiritually confused, elder warns me, "Don't get too close to her, she'll bite you."

I respond by telling them, "If she bites me, I'll knock her right out of that chair." It was time to apply the basic, biblical principles of spiritual authority.

After speaking out the same things I'm writing to you about now, I closed up my Bible and left the room. After all, even with Jesus it took a day or so for some of the people to obtain their deliverance. I had done what the Word said to do by faith, and my job was done. No, I didn't want to roll on the floor at the altar and wail. I didn't want to stay up all night in some tear-filled prayer meeting. Just apply the Word of God and go home.

> *And he said unto them, I beheld Satan as lightning fall from heaven. Behold, I give unto you power to tread on serpents and scorpions, and over all the power of the enemy: and nothing shall by any means hurt you. Notwithstanding in this rejoice not, that*

the spirits are subject unto you; but rather rejoice, because your
names are written in heaven. (Luke 10:18-20)

I beheld Satan as lightning fall from heaven. Here we go with
another major change. The enemy no longer has "throne room"
privileges. Obviously, something has changed since Job chapter
one. Whether Jesus was speaking prophetically (because this was
before he died and went to hell to defeat death, hell, and the grave)
or it was an event which happened sometime before, the result is
the same.

I (God the Father) *give you power.* Most certainly he is not
speaking of reptiles and insects. The words "serpents and scor-
pions" referred to demonic power.

So I returned, and considered all the oppressions that are done
under the sun: and behold the tears of such as were oppressed,
and they had no comforter; and on the side of their oppressors
there was power; but they had no comforter. (Ecclesiastes 4:1)

The oppressors had power—demonic power. If we do not get
a clear focus of this word *power*, we may mistakenly come away
from this verse with a misguided interpretation that one power is
very closely matched to the other power.

It gives us the picture of a very closely matched arm-wrestling
competition, where each opponent has much the same force at
his disposal. Maybe it is like the Worldwide Wrestling Federation
where the outcome of the match is determined by who wins the
first two falls out of three. Nothing could be further from the
truth. If you desire to begin to flow in the anointing and distribute
the power of God here on earth, you must operate with a rock-
solid revelation that all the power of the enemy is no match for the
anointing that resides in you.

You must develop your faith to believe that what God did in
Christ and Christ did in you is far greater than what Satan did in
Adam—or the devil has done in you, for that matter.

To successfully progress, every believer must be aware of that empowerment which enables us to overcome everything presented by the enemy. You simply must yield to the Christ in you (the Anointed One and his anointing), the hope of glory.

When the ancient English King James writers used the word *power* the first time in this verse, it is better translated *authority and force*. The second time that translators used the word, it is better translated as *abilities*. Later, Paul says that we are not ignorant of his (the devil's) devices.

Soon after Jesus empowers the seventy and further instructs them upon their return, he speaks of the strongman and the one who is stronger than he:

> *And if I by Beelzebub cast out devils, by whom do your sons cast them out? Therefore shall they be your judges. But if I with the finger of God cast out devils, no doubt the kingdom of God is come upon you. When a strong man armed keepeth his palace, his goods are in peace: But when a stronger than he shall come upon him, and overcome him, he taketh from him all his armor wherein he trusted, and divideth his spoils. (Luke 11:19-23)*

But if I with the finger (power) *of God cast out devils…the strongman, who is armed with a certain power, keepeth his palace.* Notice the choice of words:

- Palace
- Property
- Dominion
- Territory

The strongman retains his dominion over a certain territory with a measure of power. And his goods (possessions) are safe.

Who or what would these goods be if the strongman is the devil or one of his workers? Could they be believers held in bondage by sickness or disease? Or perhaps believers who are discouraged and disillusioned because of poverty and lack? You'll notice that these valuable possessions of the strongman are safe and undisturbed until verse twenty-two, *when a stronger than he shall come upon him and overcome him.*

Here is our vision for the spiritual arm-wrestling match. All of our possessions or benefits which we are entitled to receive by scripture are being withheld from us by the power (ability) of the strongman (the devil). But Praise God for when the ***stronger than he*** shows up! When the Holy Spirit's anointing is applied against the abilities (power) of the enemy, the stronger one (the Holy Spirit) overcomes the strongman (through you and me).

That's real spiritual authority. That's practical anointing!

**Transferring the Burden Removing
Yoke Destroying Anointing**

**Alright already, can you stop using
Jesus' name... we're leaving!**

This is a clear demonstration of spiritual truth. However, the application of the power of the stronger one is certainly not limited to personal deliverance. Obviously, the cleansing, delivering power of the anointing is needed and precious to us for personal deliverance. We need this anointing for the tearing down of mental strongholds, emotional strongholds, the healing of a broken heart, overcoming fears, repetitive self-destructive behavior—all these are required for true freedom and deliverance.

But consider an even larger variety of oppression which threatens the life of the believer.

It is not difficult to see in today's world the far-reaching power of the spirit of deception. In business and commerce, investment scams, forked-tongue politicians, and every other version of lying dogs, every believer has a desperate need for the anointing of the Spirit to discern good and evil and focus on the truth. After all, isn't that one of the things Jesus promised us the Comforter would do? Lead us into all truth?

> *Howbeit when he, the Spirit of truth, is come, he will guide you into all truth. (John 16:13)*

And what about the impact of the deceiver through his very popular tools—the spirits of debt, poverty, and lack? Please keep in mind that if the believer resorts to only his own natural resources, those resources will be insufficient to effectively resist the demonic attacks of the enemy. Without the personal ministry of the Greater One, the enemy with his demonic power will retain the upper hand, and true deliverance and freedom for the believer will be unobtainable.

THE PARABLE OF THE ATLANTA SPEEDWAY

Several years ago, I had the opportunity to attend a NASCAR race with some friends. We had traveled overnight to the Atlanta Motor Speedway. Our plan was to sit in the grass and watch the race from a steep hill on the backstretch.

It had rained very hard early that morning, but the track was dry and ready to race. However, the combination of the steep grade and the muddy surface created an interesting situation for us. If you sat down on the grass and dug in with your heels, you could stay in position to watch the race. But if you reclined and stretched out, gravity and the lack of friction took over and a grand slide began down to the bottom of the hill.

As we all laughed about it, the Holy Spirit spoke to me and said that this is the exact situation in the earth. We are all born on a slippery slope. This is a sin-filled, hell-dominated world. Ever since Adam and Eve granted their dominion over to the snake, the god of this world has been running much of the show. We all took our first breath in a sinful world surrounded by a majority of people whose father is the devil. We were all subject to the deteriorating, negative effects of the curse of sin.

At the NASCAR race, if we laid back in comfort to watch our amusement, the downward slide began. An old hymn came to mind about Jesus being our anchor. But if I was to make any progress going back up the hill under those slippery conditions, I would need more than an anchor.

This is a terribly revealing issue of doctrine. People rightfully believe that when they receive Christ they receive the promise of eternal life in heaven with the Father. But what about making progress going back up the hill down here on earth? The Holy Spirit was revealing to me that for us to be victorious we must walk in the power of the anointing. We simply must accept all of the precious benefits given to us by a loving God.

The sacrifice of Christ has redeemed me from the curse of the law. I have missed the devil's hell. But I also must accept the supernatural burden-removing, yoke-destroying power of God to truly enter into that overcoming lifestyle of the believer down here on earth at this time, in my lifetime, and not just expect that getting to heaven is my only "company benefit." This is how Paul can tell us a few chapters later, without qualification, that God always causes us to triumph.

> Now thanks be unto God, which always causeth us to triumph in
> Christ. (II Corinthians 2:14)

If you'll allow me to further illustrate a point, the muddy, slippery slope (the curse) is the default setting. If you fail to aggressively pursue and appropriate the blessings of God and his covenant benefits, down the slope you go. Your faith is not a passive sport. Indifference has no godly power. Indifference and procrastination hinder the power of God working in your life.

If I do not actively tell my computer what style of printing letters to use, it will automatically revert back to the default setting. Can you see the picture? Here is Jesus—he has already defeated death, hell, and the grave, and empowered us with his anointing; and when we fail to use it, that aspect of our life reverts back to the default setting. The curse is the default setting. The curse is the absence of the manifestation of covenant benefits and promises through the application of the anointing.

An inheritance must be claimed to be received by the heir. The offer of an inheritance is simply not enough. It seems very easy for most believers to see how this principle applies to salvation and eternal life. You remember the evangelist talking about the offer of the gift. The offer is made, the believer agrees to receive, and somebody gets saved. The quarterback throws the pass, and the receiver catches it.

However, some of these blessings, like healing or financial prosperity, must be aggressively and biblically pursued. You must appropriate them. You simply must learn how to get what is in the Book out of the Book and into your life. That is the walk of faith!

If free moral choice is the operating principle of God's covenant, you can no longer blame God for your failure to receive.

THE PARABLE OF THE WRENCH

Let's just say that I bought a brand-new expensive wrench at the tool store. It was made to an exacting standard, highly polished, the finest vanadium steel. Let's say I threw this wrench out in the backyard in the weeds and left it there a few years. There it was, exposed to all of the deteriorating, negative aspects of this earthly environment, and no protective measures were taken to push back this assault. The absence of my action allowed the default setting to prevail.

Without protection, without an aggressive defense against the attack, the result was the curse.

Here on our earth, just in case you haven't noticed, we have much to defend ourselves against. Many aspects of the devil's kingdom are making their combined attacks against all the aspects of our lives—spiritual, mental, physical, emotional, financial, marital, sexual, social, career, peace, family, and so forth. When we do not aggressively follow through on the victory Jesus has already gained for us in those areas, then the fruit of the devil's kingdom begins to manifest in our lives instead of the fruit Jesus promised. The default kingdom immerses us in anger, bitterness, strife, poverty, lack, deception, sickness, disease, confusion—all the demonically inspired hellish-kingdom aspects of a defeated life.

A merciful, loving God has already paid the ultimate price to display his precious love and care for us. How it must grieve his heart when he looks over the earth and sees the tears of his believers who are being oppressed by the power of the enemy, and they are doing nothing about it. They are leaving all their tools in the toolbox. Whether through ignorance or spiritual blindness, the end result is still the same.

I do not wish to enter into some denominational arm-wrestling match over what your tradition or creed book says. I simply believe that with the sheer volume and power of the available scriptures, any honest seeker will have to come to grips with his or her own spiritual component of faith. If the traditions of men have made the Word of God of no effect in your life in some particular area of doctrine, I challenge you to ask the Holy Spirit to lead you into all truth in that area. Labor in the Word on that topic. Search multiple translations. Give the Holy Spirit something to work with. If you believe scriptural truth will set you free, and you are not totally free in some area, then you just need more truth in that area.

You see, the presence and power of the anointing is not an issue for academic debate. It was not an issue for denominational debate in the days when Jesus, the flesh-and-blood man from Nazareth, walked the earth with the power of God operating in him. The religious leaders, during their interrogation of the previously blind man who was healed, insisted that he take their doctrinal stand and make some explanation in agreement with them concerning their version of the prophets and the law. His only observation was, "I was blind, but now I see." Period. The end. "I was blind, but now I see."

Understand this, as long as your discussion of the anointing remains in the academic realm, you may have your opinion, and I may have mine. Opinions are like belly buttons; everybody's got one. But if the testimony of the believer is that he was sick but now is well, if he was addicted but now is free, if she was tormented but now is at peace, you can take all your traditional, denominational, academic arguments, load them up in the closest available truck, and haul them away. If you have experienced a burden that was removed and a yoke that was destroyed, the case is closed. That is the anointing at work in the earth.

Remember this old Pentecostal axiom: *A man with a doctrine will never lord it over a man with an experience.* No carnally minded preacher and no devil from hell will ever talk you out of your next victory if you've already received one. It's too late to parachute in some guy from the home office to try and preach to me that healing isn't for today, and the biblical doctrine of prosperity doesn't work. It's too late. Those promises have already manifested.

In some ways, the believer who distributes the anointing power operates like a continuous deliverance meeting. Now some may caution and guard against seeing a demon behind every bush. I'm okay with that. But you don't have to look far in this world to see large numbers of demonically empowered people doing a full-time job of oppressing people. Just look at the current corruption in education, so-called science, and politics.

But if your doctrine is up to speed and you are on duty as God's spiritual police officer down here in the earth, no low-level devils will sneak underneath that fence into your blood-bought territory and set up their hellish kingdom in your backyard. The territory that Jesus has delivered on your behalf is your area of influence, your dominion, your home, your family, your life. Hopelessness simply doesn't apply to the anointed believer. The Word says you have to be without God in this world to have no hope. Is that really your state?

> *That at that time ye were without Christ, being aliens from the commonwealth of Israel, and strangers from the covenants of promise, having no hope, and without God in the world. (Ephesians 2:12)*

Now let's assume that situation has changed and you are now in Christ (the Anointed One and His anointing). You are in the family, positioned to receive covenant benefits, and the promises are for you (heaven, peace, abundance, healing). The Father has blessed (empowered) you with His Holy Spirit.

However, it is possible to be in the family and heaven-bound and still be a stranger to one or two of the covenants of promise. In a state of ignorance (a lack of information because you missed that class), you cannot and will not take a stand of faith for that benefit or promise to manifest. Your faith cannot rise above the known will of God.

But if you are not merely wearing the label of Christian (Little Anointed One) on your forehead, but a believer empowered by the Holy Spirit of the living God (the Greater One), then you have that power residing in you. When the enemy attacks, the outcome is assured for believers who will faithfully distribute that anointing power.

> *But if the Spirit of him that raised up Jesus from the dead dwell in you, he that raised up Christ from the dead shall also quicken your mortal bodies by his Spirit that dwelleth in you. (Romans 8:11)*

It seems some believers think the scriptures say, "He always causes us to triumph, *unless He decides to come down here and knock your block off!*"

Sorry, just had to throw that in for you extreme "sovereignty" types. Don't get me wrong, you will not find anyone more committed to believing in the sovereignty of God than I do. I truly believe that God will do exactly as he says. When he says if you do something, something else will happen, I believe it will happen, for good or for bad. That's true biblical sovereignty. That's why Jesus instructed us to seek and study the principles of the kingdom of God, how God works here on earth.

But, as in the case of any command, we all have the option of obedience. Do it or don't do it! It's up to us. That's free moral choice. That's what God gave Adam and Eve. So don't blame God for the terrible things that are brought into the earth because of the devil, our ignorance, our unbelief, or our inaction. God does his work down here through *us*.

No low level devils have authority over you if Jesus has already defeated their general. These references speak to that chain of spiritual command:

> *For we wrestle not against flesh and blood, but against principalities, against powers, against the rulers of the darkness of this world, against spiritual wickedness in high places. (Ephesians 6:12)*

> *For though we walk in the flesh, we do not war after the flesh: (For the weapons of our warfare are not carnal, but mighty through God to the pulling down of strong holds;) Casting down imaginations, and every high thing that exalteth itself against the knowledge of God, and bringing into captivity every thought to the obedience of Christ. (II Corinthians 10:3-5)*

> *For though we walk (live) in the flesh, we are not carrying on our warfare according to the flesh and using mere human weapons. For the weapons of our warfare are not physical [weapons of flesh and blood], but they are mighty before God for the overthrow and destruction of strongholds, [Inasmuch as we] refute arguments and theories and reasonings and every proud and lofty thing that sets itself up against the [true] knowledge of God; and we lead every thought and purpose away captive into the obedience of Christ (the Messiah, the Anointed one). (II Corinthians 10:3-5 AMP)*

Remember the power you have available!

You are not using mere human weapons anymore!

Flesh against demonic power equals manifestation of the curse.

Anointing against demonic power equals manifestation of the promise.

THE PARABLE OF THE FOOTBALL PLAYER AND THE GRANDMOTHER

Envision a ninety-year-old, 100-pound grandmother. Standing next to her is her twenty-year-old, 300-pound grandson, who is a champion football player. The grandson obviously has certain strengths and abilities (power) far beyond that of his grand-mother. But she has authority (power). If the young man begins to misbehave, she can and should exercise her authority to control the situation. She can loose this anointing of authority verbally by simply raising her voice and commanding him to sit! It's authority versus ability, and ability loses.

Satan, through his right of dominion received by deception from Adam and Eve, distributes these limited abilities. But we cannot blame God for our failure to receive His blessings if we don't tell the devil to sit! SIT!

In James 4, God gives us more details about the spiritual chain of command:

> But He gives us more and more grace (power of the Holy Spirit, to meet this evil tendency and all others fully). That is why He says, God sets Himself against the proud and haughty, but gives grace [continually] to the lowly (those who are humble enough to receive it). So be subject to God. Resist the devil [stand firm against him], and he will flee from you. (James 4:6,7 AMP)

Sit!

Verse seven instructs us to *resist* him and *he will flee from you*. One translation says he will run away in stark terror! It doesn't sound much like the crying of the oppressed described in Ecclesiastes 4, does it? Where is the fury of your oppressor? Where does the devil stand when it comes to you? Where do you stand when it comes to the devil? These aren't just words in some book. You have to figure out which horse you're going to ride.

Let me give you an example of practical anointing: For many years, it has been my precious honor to minister in a retirement home. Every Friday evening has been devoted to an in-depth study of the Bible during which I am surrounded by the finest, most caring and loving senior saints.

One evening, a lady about ninety-two years old came in looking very tired and distressed. She said she had been tormented each evening this week and was not able to sleep. I asked her the nature of the torment and she told me that it felt like an attack on her peace. She felt unsettled, disturbed, anxious, and somewhat fearful.

I asked her if she felt this experience was from God. "No!" She replied.

Then I asked her, "What did you do about it?" She paused and then said that she had attempted to think about good things to try and get her mind on something else. Was it effective? No, not at all.

Well, here we go again with one of my favorite slogans: *Every experience is a learning experience.*

If you just stumble along through your life and fail to truly learn how to operate in God's spiritual laws, you do not get the victories he promised.

My interest, of course, was to help my dear, sweet sister regain her peace and spend the night restfully. But as the man of God and being anointed to teach, just helping her this one time was not sufficient. She and all the other students present needed to learn how to handle these attacks from low-level tormenting devils—you know, giving them a fishing pole instead of just the fish.

Here was an opportunity to demonstrate another aspect of chain of command of spiritual authority. Thoughts versus speech versus action. There is a hierarchy of spiritual authority. The word spoken by a born-again, Bible-believing, Holy Spirit-empowered believer has a greater level of spiritual authority than just a thought.

The instruction for her was this: As she returned to her apartment that night to sleep, immediately upon the onset of the demonic torment, she was to spin around off her bed, stand up, point her finger like she was lecturing a poorly behaved child, and begin to speak these words out loud:

"You low-level, tormenting devils, I take authority over you in the strong name of Jesus of Nazareth. I plead the blood of Jesus against you. The Word of God says that when I resist you, you shall flee from me. In the name of Jesus, as it is written, so let it be done. Be gone and leave me alone. Now precious Holy Spirit, in faith I receive the peace that Jesus has given me."

She followed my instruction, got back into bed, drifted off, and slept like a baby. When we all gathered around the Word again the following Friday night, it was a night of great rejoicing and celebration.

The Word of God works when you work the Word of God.

In my course called Faith School, we make it a practice of saying out loud our faith-filled confessions. You may have heard some of these examples before:

I am who God says I am.
I can do what God says I can do.
I can be what God says I can be.
I can have what God says I can have.

Believe me, these powerful, faith-filled words are the last thing the devil and his workers want to hear coming out of the anointed mouth of a covenant-believer.

We resist the enemy with the tools given to us as described in the Bible:

- The name of Jesus of Nazareth
- The power of the blood of Jesus
- The anointed Word of God
- Dispatching angels to work on our behalf

We are to use all of the resources God has given us. To obtain and maintain the promises and covenant benefits he has provided for us, we must respond against the attacks of the devil with overwhelming firepower. Resisting the devil is not a fair fight. He doesn't have a chance against The Father, The Son, and the Holy

Spirit working through the anointed believer. God didn't design the system to be fair against the devil. It's not even close to a fair fight.

For far too long, the church has not properly recognized the enormous power contained in the spoken word of God coming out of the mouth of an anointed believer. In First Thessalonians 2:13, the word is described as exercising its superhuman power in those who adhere to and trust in and rely on it:

> *And we also [especially] thank God continually for this, that when you received the message of God [which you heard] from us, you welcomed it not as the word of [mere] men, but as it truly is, the Word of God, which is effectually at work in you who believe [exercising its superhuman power in those who adhere to and trust in and rely on it]. (I Thessalonians 2:13 AMP)*

So many of the day-to-day situations in life can be handled easily by a believer walking in revelatory knowledge and exercising his high privilege of distributing the anointing.

Let me show you another example of practical anointing and the authority of the believer.

Over my lifetime, my body had been victimized by a recurring attack in my throat area. Whether this attack has come to me bearing the name of sore throat, a cold, strep throat, the flu, or any other name, I know now that the name of Jesus is far above every name, including that one.

> *Wherefore God also hath highly exalted him, and given him a name which is above every name. (Philippians 2:9)*

As a babe in Christ, I was ignorant of the power that resided in me. I was in the family but a stranger to the covenant. Nearly every time this symptom appeared in my throat, I would have to wait out the recovery of my body sometimes for days and sometimes for weeks. In other words, the outcome I expected was the same outcome that every member of God's creation could expect instead of the outcome of a Family member.

God's creation includes everybody—all believers, unbelievers, heathens, Buddhists, Muslims, atheists, and devil worshippers of every description. His *family* is a very different group. I expected no special benefit whatsoever from being a member of the family of God (ignorance), no special treatment by a loving Father, no practical benefit here in this earth from my personal relationship with the Christ (the Anointed One and his anointing). After all, some preacher told me that it would all get better over on the other side.

Here's another one of my favorite slogans: *Thank God there is a cure for ignorance.*

Ignorance is just the absence of information. In my case, it was the truth of the Word of God concerning healing. I had just missed a few lessons. I'm not stupid. I had just missed the classes on spiritual authority, the anointing, and healing.

Don't come under condemnation here; missing classes is a popular disease in the church. With some time, training resources, and the leadership of the Holy Spirit, you can make up those classes you missed and get yourself trained in the covenant in any area which is new to you.

After the entrance of revelatory knowledge in this area, a new set of expectations and confessions became my normal course of action. At the first indication of that little tickle in my throat, at that very second, I respond to the attack with overwhelming firepower—that is, in the spiritual realm.

Here is the confession I declared out loud:

"You trespassing, microscopic organisms attempting to set up a stronghold of symptoms in my body, I curse you at the root and I command you to dry up and die. Be removed and be cast into the sea in Jesus' name. Sickness and disease, you shall not lord it over me. Satan, you have no power or authority over me. Your attack on me shall not prevail. I plead the blood of Jesus against you, and I resist you. The Word of God says that when I resist you, you shall flee from me. As it is written, so let it be done in Jesus' name. Now precious Holy Spirit, by faith I loose that anointing within me to heal, to remove every burden, and destroy every yoke. And by faith I receive my healing that Jesus provided for me on the cross 2,000 years ago."

I can tell you from personal experience that multiple attacks of this nature over the years have been successfully defended. The job for the believer is to absolutely refuse to accept delivery of any aspect of Satan's hellish kingdom. So when you hear the devil's dump truck backing up in your front yard (beep, beep, beep), just stand to your feet as an anointed, empowered believer, and refuse to take delivery from him.

Is your confession like King David's?

> *For who is this uncircumcised Philistine, that he should defy the armies of the living God? (I Samuel 17:26)*

Do it immediately upon sensing the attack! It reminds me of what my sister and ministry partner Joyce Meyer has taught. Don't wait till it takes three busloads of Christians to pray you out of your problem. Take that shield of faith which Paul teaches us about and quench that fiery dart (defense). Then stand up and use that sword (offense)!

- Let correct covenant words come out of that mouth of yours!
- Use your mouth as a faith tool!
- Use your faith as a tool!
- Use the Word of God against the devil and see what happens!

> *Above all, taking the shield of faith, wherewith ye shall be able to quench all the fiery darts of the wicked. And take the helmet of salvation, and the sword of the Spirit, which is the word of God. (Ephesians 6:16,17)*

Lift up over all the [covering] shield of saving faith, upon which you can quench all the flaming missiles of the wicked [one]. And take the helmet of salvation and the sword that the Spirit wields, which is the Word of God. (Ephesians 6:16,17 AMP)

VALUABLE LESSONS LEARNED

Many lessons learned in security- and self-defense training in the natural realm reflect powerful spiritual principles. For many years, it has been my privilege to receive and give specialized self-defense firearm training. I have had some excellent instructors. They have instilled in me a series of well-established priorities, the first one being firearm safety.

You never want to hurt anyone by accident whom you don't want to hurt on purpose. There is no such thing as an accident with a gun. When you are dealing with any weapon capable of producing deadly force, safety is the number one issue. Handling each weapon properly and carefully, knowing its correct operation, always observing the basic lesson of not pointing the weapon at anything or anyone whom you do not intend to shoot…all these teaching principles lead to a lifetime of safe gun handling. Once that level of safety training is established, it's time to examine the principles of self-defense.

The priorities can be listed as follows:

1. Safety
2. Target identification
3. Accuracy
4. Speed
5. Distance
6. Multiple targets

A properly armed self-defense plan follows those priorities like a checklist:

1. Safety is always first.
2. There are no accidents.
3. Know exactly what you're doing, or don't do it.
4. Get proper training.
5. No exceptions.

TARGET IDENTIFICATION

Identify the threat level presented by the target. Obviously, an unarmed man who is falling-down drunk and stumbling over himself does not present the same threat level as an armed man intent on harming you or yours. Once the threat level has been evaluated, it is time for you to respond in a manner appropriate to the threat. In this politically correct world, the liberal elite governing class would like your only option to be calling 911 and waiting for the "proper" authorities to handle every situation. (Don't get me started about the continuous assault on my Second Amendment right to self-defense described in **MY** Constitution. The right of self-defense as well as all the others comes from Almighty God and not from any government.)

ACCURACY

I am in favor of gun control. Gun control means hitting what you aim at with every round.

Here's a good place for a real-world story about accuracy. Early one morning, as my plane landed in Baltimore, the TV news blared the details of a big gang shoot-out which had happened the night before.

Law enforcement officers had counted over 200 shots fired by the opposing gang members in a gun battle which lasted about thirty minutes. There were no deaths and no one was even injured. Not one of the 200-plus rounds had hit its target. Fortunately for all concerned, these inner city criminals never bothered to take the time for proper training.

While we're here, let's sort through some present-day nonsense. Do you want to speculate on how these hoodlums obtained those guns? Do you believe they have a deep reverence and respect for the law and filled out all the proper firearms-purchase paperwork that a law-abiding citizen is expected to do? Do you honestly think additional gun laws against the possession of firearms would have had any effect on these people?

SPEED

Rapid fire of any weapon is a useless defense without accuracy. Rapid fire with accuracy eliminates the threat more quickly, thus reducing the risk to you and those whom you defend.

DISTANCE

By its very definition, distance may reduce the true threat level. An attacker with a two-inch barrel, small-caliber handgun, standing four blocks away, hollering at you and shooting up into the air is not an immediate threat to you. The correct civilian response would be to take cover and monitor the threat while trying to avoid any further confrontation, and leave the scene immediately.

FBI reports reveal that the vast majority of all civilian gunfights happen within six feet between the participants, and most begin within thirty seconds after the initial face-to-face meeting. Distance is your friend when you need to retreat.

MULTIPLE TARGETS

Most armed civilian self-defense situations do not include more than one attacker. However, complete self-defense training should include your effective response to multiple targets. Our FBI teaches that you shoot the guy who's holding the shotgun first. He represents the greatest danger in a close-quarters gunfight.

If the target presents immediate life-threatening harm, you must respond with overwhelming firepower. In terms of self-defense with a firearm, overwhelming firepower means you repeatedly concentrate your fire on the target until you are no longer able to do so (out of ammunition).

Note: A violent confrontation is real life-and-death stuff. This is not the movies. You do not cease fire because the target has fallen to the ground, or appears to have stopped moving momentarily, or his gun might be jammed, or he appears to have lowered his weapon. You continue to fire until you have no more rounds in your weapon.

When your weapon is empty, you immediately seek cover and reload. Then begins the continued process of identification and evaluation of any remaining threat, and the checklist begins all over again.

Remember, the point of self-defense training is first to avoid the threat, if at all possible. If avoidance is not possible, then self-defense training teaches you to eliminate the threat.

1. Identify the threat.
2. Respond with overwhelming firepower (continue until weapon is empty).
3. Seek cover.
4. Reload and prepare to continue your self-defense, if needed.

Now a special word to you nonviolent-at-any-cost types. When I speak about violence in this context, I am not talking about a nonviolent march to protest some political issue or to demand a social or government response to a problem. I am talking about an evil, life-threatening attack against you and your family.

Jesus and my brother and ministry partner Paul teach me that, if at all possible, I should be at peace with all men. This policy of nonviolence has been adopted for my life. That means I will defer to ignorance, drunkenness, belligerence, outspoken prejudice, race-baiting, harassment, anti-Semitic speech, world-class ignorance, Christian-hating, socialist trade-union bullying, and every other form of non-life-threatening verbal abuse or any other attempt at intimidation against myself and my family. I am committed to use every resource within my being to avoid that situation escalating up to violence, especially armed violence. That includes making deliberate decisions to avoid unnecessary confrontations with the ignorant.

It certainly includes the useful option of simply walking away, even when my manhood is questioned, or my wife has been insulted, or having been called a coward or any other name. Not only do we not pick fights, but we attempt to bring peace into every situation. However, in this sin-filled world, which is highly populated with demonically inspired, armed bad guys, such a choice is not always possible.

I believe there is nothing in scripture, either old or new covenant, which requires that a believer stand by helplessly as a mere witness or victim to a physical life-threatening attack against himself or his family without exercising his God-given right of self-defense.

Please note, this a personal policy as well as a national government policy.

A gun is a tool. My checkbook is a tool. My vote is a tool. I will use each in its appropriate application of force and power against ungodly behavior whenever needed.

Since we went down this rabbit trail about gun use and gun safety, let me throw in a few extra points. Keeping a firearm in your home is, by its very presence, dangerous. It exposes you and others to possible harm. Keeping the weapon out of the hands of the untrained is paramount. Children should be taught what to do if a firearm is discovered, wherever it is found. In today's culture, this training is not an option but a life-saving necessity. Whenever and wherever a gun is discovered, your children should know to not touch it, to leave the room immediately, and then go and tell an adult. It is your responsibility to conduct such training *whether you keep firearms or not,* regardless of your philosophical outlook. Gun owners must keep each weapon secured from unintended use. Excellent firearm safety materials are available from the National Rifle Association.

Now the parallel truth.

When confronted with an attack of some hellish aspect of Satan's kingdom, I must push you a little further and get you to answer this question: *What will make you fight?* I see so many people in the church who passively accept Satan's delivery of the negative, destructive aspects of his hellish kingdom into their lives without even putting up a fight.

That blind acceptance of the manifestation of the curse often comes from their confused error-filled doctrine concerning free moral choice and the "so-called" sovereignty of God. Some believers are so confused about life, they actually believe everything that happens down here on earth is not only pleasing to God but it's part of his divine plan. From Adam and Eve's big mistake to every fatal truck wreck, that cancer, your relatives going to hell without knowing Jesus, it's all just a part of his plan...

Dear God, please forgive them—they know not what they do.

Those people who are in the ditch about this perverted version of God's sovereignty will have great difficulty receiving anything good from God. Those folks will never know if they should resist it or not. They don't know the origin of what is presented to them in life, so they are uncertain as to their response to it.

Hatred, bitterness, striving, anger, deception, sickness, disease, poverty, lack, torment, worry, unease, hopelessness, grief, fear, going to hell, the list goes on. What are you willing to accept? What is it that will finally make you stand up and fight?

What will cause you to respond with overwhelming spiritual firepower? What aspects of Satan's hellish kingdom has he been delivering unopposed into your life? Have you failed to exercise your God-given right of self-defense against your enemies? Did you miss the valuable training about how to deliver up the anointing?

The Father has paid a heavy price to secure your high privilege to possess and distribute the anointing. Maybe it's time for you to take some self-defense classes, both spiritual and natural. The Word tells us that we are not ignorant of his (Satan's) devices:

> *Lest Satan should get an advantage of us: for we are not ignorant of his devices. (II Corinthians 2:11)*

> *To keep Satan from getting the advantage over us; for we are not ignorant of his wiles and intentions. (II Corinthians 2:11 AMP)*

If you're honest with yourself and the Holy Spirit, you should be able to prepare a short list of those avenues of access which the enemy has used in the past to deliver his oppression into your life. Perhaps it's your finances or maybe a bad back. Maybe the enemy chooses to attack you through your children's behavior or through a disloyal person at work. Maybe it's through chronic sickness or heartbreak over the wayward life of a loved one.

Identify and evaluate the source and threat level of the attack focused against you and learn how to respond with the overwhelming firepower of the anointing and the Word of God. For the fulfillment of your spiritual destiny, you had better find out what will make you exercise your spiritual authority! For the fulfillment of your spiritual destiny, make it a priority to find out what will make you stand up and fight!

A SINGLE MOTHER AND THE DRUG HOUSE

There was a precious, young, single mom who came to my Bible study classes a few years back. Her useless, sorry husband had run off sometime before. She and her children lived in a rental house in a bad part of town.

She told me that there was an active drug house right across the street, and that dealers and customers of every description would come and go all night long. Some of the visitors looked like they lived in their clothes and slept in a cardboard box, and some came in fancy cars with expensive metal briefcases.

After contacting the local city police (that's responding in the natural), she was told that they could do nothing unless someone was arrested with drugs in his possession. (In other words, she responded only in the natural realm.) After explaining the situation to me, she asked what she could do about this problem, which was endangering her young family and her neighborhood. I encouraged her to take a direction that was the exclusive territory of a faith-filled believer. After all, any heathen can call 911, but God's supernatural resources are reserved exclusively for covenant people.

SATAN IN THE SIGHTS

I asked her, "What weapons do you have, and what resources can you draw on as a covenant believer? The name of Jesus, the blood of Jesus, the anointing of the Holy Spirit, mighty warring angels sent to labor on our behalf, anointing with oil, prayer cloths? These are just some of your options. If you are at peace with this course of action, then why don't you take these steps?

"Walk the boundaries of your property and re-establish the bloodline. Declare that Jesus' blood bought hedge of protection over your particular dominion. Take authority over the neighborhood, and bind the demonic spirits with the powerful name of Jesus, the name which is above every name.

"When there's no activity at the house (let's face it, most drug dealers are sound asleep at five or six o'clock in the morning!), take your bottle of anointing oil and anoint the doorposts of the drug house.

"Walk around the house, and place anointed prayer cloths on the property. Continue your walk around the neighborhood, distributing anointed prayer cloths and thanking God for the unusual manifestations of his love and power through this unusual instrumentality."

> So that from his body were brought unto the sick handkerchiefs or aprons, and the diseases departed from them, and the evil spirits went out of them. (Acts 19:12)

> And God did unusual and extraordinary miracles by the hands of Paul, So that handkerchiefs or towels or aprons which had touched his skin were carried away and put upon the sick, and their diseases left them and the evil spirits came out of them. (Acts 19:11,12 AMP)

Now don't you dare go out and tell your pastor that Brother David says to take on the drug lords single-handedly. Don't use me or this bold young lady as your example. You must be at peace with the Holy Spirit for your own selection of actions.

But don't just sit passively by and let the devil conduct his evil work unopposed. If you're fearful, your first thoughts probably were, *Did she get shot?* Or you might say, "I'd be too scared to do that," or some other fear-based confession.

Those of you who are experienced in the walk of faith already know the outcome of this drama. The lady came back the following week with the most dramatic testimony. The day after her actions were taken, the cops arrested several bad guys at the house. Yellow tape was set up all around the drug house property. Regular police patrols began to appear by day and by night.

In a day or so, all of the government suits and ties appeared and had a media meeting on the front porch of the drug house. Two days later, a bulldozer leveled the house and a dump truck hauled away the debris. The city fathers announced a plan for a small neighborhood park.

God is so fabulous, he is so good, and he is waiting for us to take action as his ambassadors. After all, we are his light. He is planning on us to do our jobs empowered with his help.

That experience marked the life of a young, single mother, and the telling of that story has inspired many believers to move up to a new level of spiritual authority. Remember, we all are a walking Bible story.

With regard to the relative power of various instrumentalities, consider the power of flesh versus spiritual power. Concerning addictions, you can go to all the twelve-step programs in existence to combat your particular challenge, but unless and until you confront the power of the flesh and demonic oppression with a superior force (Holy Spirit spiritual force), you will be led around through life responding to every demand of the flesh, whether it's food, sex, drugs, debt, booze, hate, violence, or some other destructive pattern.

Can you see it? Good, moral people with problems can attempt to oppose demonic spiritual power, but no amount of personal discipline or "will power" will bring about the victory. Spiritual power is superior to natural or fleshly power. God demands you think this out!

Why do bad things happen to good people? I can save you a lot of headaches and countless hours reading those "just hang on" self-help books. It's the devil! A natural force applied against a spiritual force will fail every time. Is it any wonder we see countless well-meaning, heaven-bound believers who are so easily defeated by demonic opposition due to their poor New Testament training? They have no revelatory knowledge of Who (the Greater One) is within them.

Now let's look at the other side of this. Can you see even the most nominal believer with a beginning revelation of spiritual authority empowered by the personal ministry of the Holy Spirit standing his ground against a demonic attack manifesting itself in the natural realm? What do you think the laying on of hands is all about? It's our natural flesh anointed by God to change things here in the natural. That's the reverse of Satan using his demonic power to affect our natural flesh and our earthly surroundings.

So, if flesh cannot stand against spirit, and the Holy Spirit who dwells within us is the Greater One, where does that leave the devil and his crowd when it's time for you to fight?

> *Ye are of God, little children, and have overcome them: because greater is he that is in you, than he that is in the world. (I John 4:4)*

How are you enjoying your steak meal?
I guarantee you that the Word of God is a steak lover's paradise. It's the food you crave using the highest-quality ingredients! Ready for more? Let's go!

CHAPTER 8

TRUE CHRISTIAN
SUFFERING

I might as well get this right out on the table here and now. Sometimes folks think they are having a genuine Christian-life experience down here on earth, when all they really have is a cheap imitation with no spiritual depth whatsoever.

What am I talking about?

Well, much of what I see believers calling "suffering for Jesus" is just people failing at the important issues of life and death here on earth. It's due to many causes—poor New Testament covenant training, the traditions of men, deception, fear, and misinformation. You can't go through life blaming the devil for acting every time he sees an opening in your life. That's *his* job.

I really can't take the time within the scope of this book to teach the reality and truth found in the book of Job. If you have suffered under a misguided, error-filled teaching about God destroying

Job for no reason other than a whim and Job having no recourse except to hang on tight till it's over, you need light and truth in this area. With only room and time for a short couple of points, just consider this. Heaven help you if you are one of those who thinks, *You never know what God is going to do.*

If Job did nothing wrong, why did he have to repent? Exactly what did he have to repent of? If that traditional interpretation of the book of Job is true and Job did not do anything wrong, yet God destroyed him for no reason and God is still doing it this way today (irrational selective destruction), where is the double restoration in the lives of believers who have had great tragedy come into their lives? I mean, if this is how God really does his business with us, shouldn't we see the same result—the double restoration? If light and truth haven't come to you to settle the great doctrinal argument of free moral choice versus the sovereignty of God, you may still be siding with the view that God is exclusively in charge of all that ever happens to you. Come on, you preacher-types who have been explaining away every bad outcome in a believer's life experience as some cosmic perfect will of God that we're really not supposed to understand. If everything that happens in the earth is his will, then you have no more input into the outcome of your life than a marionette puppet on the end of a string. If that is the case, you really don't have a clue about the dominion the Father vested in Adam and Eve and why it was so imperative that Jesus went to hell, defeated Satan, recaptured the dominion given to God's creation, restored it back to us, and showed us how to use it down here on earth to establish his kingdom.

Take that kind of misguided thinking, throw in a little error-filled doctrine concerning predestination, and you will have the most placid, inactive, inefficient, passive, ineffective, non-fruit-bearing, fear-filled, time-wasting, program-inventing, group of people who call themselves the church. Are you getting the idea? I'm not happy to say that this description applies to much of the contemporary church. It doesn't sound much like "more than overcomers" to me; does it to you?

Think about this: Some of the great Eastern religions contain this same level of confusion and spiritual ignorance between God being both good and evil at the same time. All we need to do is look to the demonic Hindu god, Shiva, the destroyer Kali, the source of regenerative life and destruction at the same time. Hindus teach that their god may grant you a bountiful harvest and then send a storm to destroy it. If you travel to various churches as I do, you'll hear some of that doctrine from behind the pulpit. It's insulting to God. After all, not being able to tell the difference is exactly what Job had to repent of.

If you still believe that God uses the devil as a subcontractor to punish or teach you something, frankly, it will be extremely difficult for you to take an effective stand of faith to receive that which the Father has promised to you and Jesus has already paid for you to have.

Many in the church are quite comfortable accusing their Father of being a child abuser. Just think about it. Some people's understanding of God leads them to conclude that from time to time, the Father will sic the devil on you like a pit bull dog on a mailman. Like Al Capone used Frank Nitty as an enforcer.

Can you imagine at the end of time the Father explaining to his children that neither he, the Son, the Holy Spirit, the anointing, 6,000 years of recorded history, seventeen translations, the Amplified Bible, twenty-four-hour-per-day Christian television, 200 hours of Fred Price tapes—all of these resources were insufficient to teach us. He just had to hire the evil one on a part-time basis as a substitute teacher, since none of his heavenly resources were apparently able to get the job done. Do you really believe that to be the case? The devil has used that deception to spread his cause and used that doctrine since the Garden of Eden.

Here are some examples of confessions which reveal the highest order of spiritual ignorance:

- "God made me sick to teach me something."
- "Miracles are just not for today."
- "Healing passed away with the death of the last apostle."
- "All of the men in my family have sugar diabetes; I guess I am no different."
- "The Bible can't be taken literally."
- "I guess we'll just never get out of debt."
- "God must love poor people because he made so many of them."
- "I guess we're just not supposed to have anything."
- "I get the flu about this time every year."
- "All of the houses in our neighborhood are getting broken into; I guess ours will be next."
- "Everybody has to die of something."
- "They're laying off down at the plant; I guess I'll be next."

Hello! Is anybody getting this?

The principle of positive, faith-filled confessions is a rudimentary and foundational principle in any study of faith. (For more details, see upcoming book titled *Faith School*.)

For now, I hope that this instructional book on the anointing is not your first excursion into the faith principles taught in scripture. It would have been better that you had successfully passed Faith School as your first prerequisite to this study on the anointing.

My brother and ministry partner Creflo Dollar has described true Christian suffering as the fight to maintain what Jesus has already obtained for you. The suffering of believers occurs when they are resisting everything which Jesus already bore for us on the cross.

> *Surely he hath borne our griefs, and carried our sorrows: yet we did esteem him stricken, smitten of God, and afflicted. But he was wounded for our transgressions, he was bruised for our iniq-*

uities: the chastisement of our peace was upon him; and with his stripes we are healed. All we like sheep have gone astray; we have turned every one to his own way; and the LORD hath laid on him the iniquity of us all. (Isaiah 53:4-6)

God the Father has already paid the ultimate price in the sacrifice of Jesus for our sins to be removed from our lives and made us qualified for entrance into heaven and eternal life. Besides the sin, what else did Jesus bear?

Surely He has borne our griefs (sicknesses, weaknesses, and distresses) and carried our sorrows and pains [of punishment], yet we [ignorantly] considered Him stricken, smitten, and afflicted by God [as if with leprosy]. [Matt 8:17] But He was wounded for our transgressions, He was bruised for our guilt and iniquities; the chastisement [needful to obtain] peace and well-being for us was upon Him, and with the stripes [that wounded] Him we are healed and made whole. He was oppressed, [yet when] He was afflicted, He was submissive and opened not His mouth; like a lamb that is led to the slaughter, and as a sheep before her shearers is dumb, so He opened not His mouth. (Isaiah 53:4-5,7 AMP)

The Amplified Bible gives us a list of things that Jesus bore for us: grief, sickness, weakness, distress, sorrow, pain, transgression, guilt, iniquity, going astray, oppression, affliction, death, wickedness, and sin.

So your part in true Christian suffering when confronted by these things, which Jesus already bore, is to by faith apply the anointing and overcome the circumstances. Overcoming it includes passing through without the negative, destructive forces of the enemy gaining ultimate victory. Either way, it's walking with God on your side with his power and his favor operating on your behalf.

You see, without walking in revelation, tradition says that our suffering automatically leads to defeat. True Christian suffering never carries with it the implication of defeat. Remember the "through the valley of the shadow of death" thing? *Through!* Don't camp out there so long you begin to learn how death does his stuff! Walk in how God does *his* stuff!

Philippians 3:13 is my part in walking in his resurrection power:

> *Brethren, I count not myself to have apprehended: but this one thing I do, forgetting those things which are behind, and reaching forth unto those things which are before, I press toward the mark for the prize of the high calling of God in Christ Jesus. (Philippians 3:13)*

Jesus shed his blood to get rid of yesterday! Forgetting those things which are behind is my part. I press toward the mark or the goal. Thank God my past and all of its failures are under the Blood. Are yours? Well, start to act like it! Use the anointing to break those bonds.

Suffering may include staying where God planted me, learning to overcome those obstacles and challenges that are presented during my life down here in a sin-filled world. But the victory contained in true Christian suffering always has the seeds of promotion. If you stand strong on the word of God in your walk of faith during your personal battle with any form of the devil's oppression, you become hardened to difficulty and more skillful in walking in the anointing. But be careful here! Don't invent yet another error-filled doctrine. Adversity is not the teacher. Contrary to popular belief, experience is not the best teacher. The Word of God and the personal witness of the Holy Spirit are the finest resources available for our spiritual education.

Now here is another one of those favorite sayings:

Every experience is a learning experience.

The point is that, as a Christian, you should be learning how to overcome and triumph. Remember the Word says be thankful <u>in</u> all things, not <u>for</u> all things. I am not thankful for that which

Satan attempts to bring into my life. (I know this is tough for you sold-out sovereignty types.) When I am under an attack of oppression of whatever nature, I am thankful to God for the resources he has given me for victory.

> *But the God of all grace, who hath called us unto his eternal glory by Christ Jesus, after that ye have suffered a while, make you perfect, stablish, strengthen, settle you. To him be glory and dominion for ever and ever. Amen. (I Peter 5:10,11)*

All adversity does is give the chance for an accomplished faith-believer to demonstrate the love of God, his heart of goodness, the absolute truth of his Word, and the unmatched power of the personal ministry of the Holy Spirit at work in our lives. The outcome should be no different than when Jesus resisted the devil.

> *Fear thou not; for I am with thee: be not dismayed; for I am thy God: I will strengthen thee; yea, I will help thee; yea, I will uphold thee with the right hand of my righteousness. Behold, all they that were incensed against thee shall be ashamed and confounded: they shall be as nothing; and they that strive with thee shall perish. Thou shalt seek them, and shalt not find them, even them that contended with thee: they that war against thee shall be as nothing, and as a thing of nought. For I the LORD thy God will hold thy right hand, saying unto thee, Fear not; I will help thee. (Isaiah 41:10-13)*

True Christian suffering is doing what he said to get what he told you that you could have. It's fighting the good fight of faith and resisting the enemy to maintain what Jesus already obtained.

True Christian suffering is simply for us to continue the battle to retain what he has already gained for us on the cross.

Here's another way you can look at our situation during hard times: When I enter the boxing ring with the devil and all of the hellish aspects of his kingdom, I am not there to contend for the victory. That victory has already been won by Jesus, my Lord.

My job is simply to reinforce the victory Jesus gained over the devil 2,000 years ago.

> *Strengthened with all might, according to his glorious power, unto all patience and longsuffering with joyfulness; Giving thanks unto the Father, which hath made us meet to be partakers of the inheritance of the saints in light: Who hath delivered us from the power of darkness, and hath translated us into the kingdom of his dear Son. (Colossians 1:11-13)*

Strengthened with all might according to his glorious power! Look out, devil! There's the anointing kicking in! Giving thanks unto the Father, who's made us meet to be partakers of the inheritance of the saints and light.

The ancient English King James version uses the word "meet," which is better translated to our word "able." It implies a qualification. And the word "partaker" is much better translated as "partner." Read it that way, that God has made us able to be partners in the inheritance. Oh, do you remember Acts 26 and Paul's job description?

> *To open their eyes, and to turn them from darkness to light, and from the power of Satan unto God, that they may receive forgiveness of sins, and inheritance among them which are sanctified by faith that is in me. (Acts 26:18)*

Get them into the family and teach them about their inheritance. One of the many wonderful aspects of our inheritance is the personal ministry of the Holy Spirit and the anointing active in our lives.

"Who hath delivered us from the power of darkness and hath translated us into the kingdom of his dear son." I mean, let's really get down to brass tacks here. Do you honestly believe that God sent Jesus to deliver us from the power of the devil, and then on those certain days when he gets out of bed and just feels a little out of sorts, he gets on the telephone with the devil and instructs him to come and afflict us and bring about our destruction by the very instrumentalities which Jesus bore on the cross and then provided the anointing to overcome? I mean, this is really where the rubber meets the road for believers and their core doctrine.

So let me ask it again: Do you honestly believe that God sent Jesus to deliver us from the power of the devil, and then on those certain days when he gets out of bed and just feels a little out of sorts, he gets on the telephone with the devil and instructs him to come and afflict us and bring about our destruction by the very instrumentalities which Jesus bore on the cross (poverty, sickness, death, etc.) and then provided for us the anointing to overcome?

You are simply going to have to decide which horse you are going to ride.

The age-old argument between free moral choice and the sovereignty of God has to get personal for you. The choice must be made by you and only you. Your decision is imperative in this matter. The fulfillment of your spiritual destiny hangs in the balance. The word of God says that God is Love. Do you believe that Love will, on a whim, violate his covenant promise of protection and blessing and favor and elect to come down here and knock your block off for no apparent reason?

This matter must be settled with all finality once and for all for your walk of faith to successfully receive that which the Father has paid such a heavy price for you to inherit.

I have heard it said that the believer has a special form of diplomatic immunity down here on earth. That's a good way to look at it. You need to understand the spiritual chain of command and how that applies to the believer to properly determine your options in the suffering issue. God granted Adam and Eve dominion over the earth. (Dear God, we need to do a serious study on our dominion.)

They disobeyed God, sin entered the earth, and the dominion was transferred over to the snake. Satan then had legal authority to develop all of his various burdens and yokes. Then Jesus came and defeated death, hell, the grave, and, as John tells us, destroyed all of the works of the devil.

> *He that committeth sin is of the devil; for the devil sinneth from the beginning. For this purpose the Son of God was manifested, that he might destroy the works of the devil. (I John 3:8)*

Watch this principal very carefully. The devil still has a legal right to be in the earth and attempt to deliver his oppressions. For the believer, skilled in the Word of God and empowered by the Anointed One and his anointing, those attacks have no legal right to prevail. That is what your resisting is all about. The attacker has no legal right to prevail against you.

Let's touch on something else that will affect your long-term outlook about the anointing. How can you explain situations and circumstances where the anointing does not appear to work?

What if we fail to receive a promise—for example, healing. Some ministers base their whole doctrine on this exception to the rule. The reality is not everyone who is offered a gift agrees to receive it. Some have not met the biblical conditions of the transfer. We certainly don't know everything about the circumstances. The people who did not receive may not know, but God knows. At the risk of being called an eternal optimist (a true faith-man), I choose to focus on the countless numbers of people who **have** received that which God has promised them. Every giving of a message does not result in every single hearer accepting Christ. Maybe that day will come. Every healing message does not result in one hundred percent effectiveness against every disease. Maybe that day will come too. But rather than focusing on the exceptions to the rule, we need to zero in on the revelatory knowledge God has already given us. Receiving and flowing in the anointing is a terribly personal issue. Although I deeply love my brothers and sisters in the Lord, my attention should be drawn to identifying the hindrances in my life which prohibit the transfer of the anointing, and not be concerned so much with other people's business. This is not an attitude of indifference. It simply means that I will be blessed with a much greater insight into the anointing and how to flow in it if I can identify and remove those issues from my life which keep me from receiving. Armed with that spiritual skill, I can then move on to help others.

In the next chapter we will talk about the anointing in the life of Jesus. Nowhere on the earth will you find a story like this one! When the Word of God was put into print in your language for you to read, God presented you with a plan for living that cost him everything and cost us nothing but faith to receive it. No one else can match this offer. It will inspire you to come back for more! Let's go!

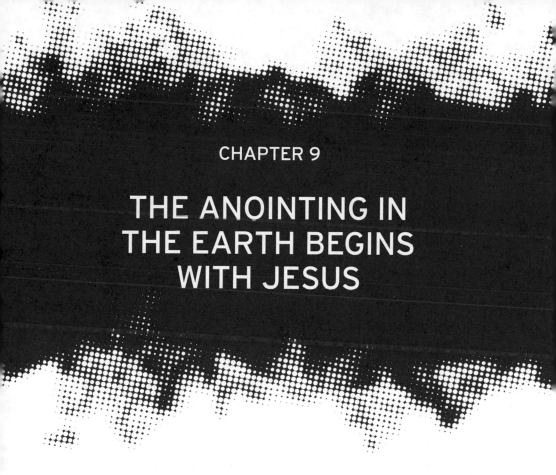

CHAPTER 9

THE ANOINTING IN THE EARTH BEGINS WITH JESUS

So I returned, and considered all the oppressions that are done under the sun: and behold the tears of such as were oppressed, and they had no comforter; and on the side of their oppressors there was power; but they had no comforter. (Ecclesiastes 4:1)

King Solomon has just returned from his world tour observing all the activities of the earth. Here we have the wisest man in the world seeing that many people are in tears from the weight of oppression that is crushing them.

My old Webster's Dictionary describes oppression in several ways: *to weigh heavily on the mind, spirits, or senses* (see our soul, spirit, body being subject to oppression?); *a burden; to keep down by the cruel or unjust use of power or authority* (doesn't that sound just like the devil and his deception?); *burden with harsh, rigorous impositions; tyrannize over; to crush* (Luke 4 checklist word is *bruised*); *to trample down; to overpower or subdue.*

I'm known as a stickler for the meaning of words, insisting to know what they really stand for. If you don't, you'll accept it when some forked-tongue politician redefines your government-imposed taxes as "an investment" or "your contribution"; or some sexual perversion as an "alternative lifestyle"; or pleading "not guilty" as meaning they didn't do it instead of the real truth being you just can't prove it in a court of law; or the pronouncements of a so-called "unbiased media," when in fact it is the public opinion manipulation industry.

To deceive means *to ensnare; to make a person believe what is not true; delude; mislead; deliberate misrepresentation of facts by words, actions, etc.; to cause to follow the wrong course; to present a false promise; to trick one to believe an illusion or fraud.*

The devil is the original liar. His deception started with lying to Eve and took off from there. Don't be surprised if his children (the majority of people here on earth) have gotten real good at it. Lying is their way of life, but you don't need to fall for it.

> *And the serpent said unto the woman, Ye shall not surely die.*
> *(Genesis 3:4)*

Solomon also observes, that they (the ones who were being oppressed) have no comforter. He further recognizes that on the side of the oppressors there was power (demonic power). Those applying that demonic power caused the people under oppression to cry.

That sounds like a very accurate observation of our present day.

The word "comfort" or "comforter" means *to make strong; to soothe and provide relief in distress, sorrow or grief; to bring about a state of ease and quiet enjoyment, free from worry or pain; make life easy and comfortable; a mitigation; at ease in body and mind; the absence of disturbing, painful, or distressing features of life; contentment; freedom of care; shelter against a storm; brings freedom.*

The word "power" means *the ability to control others' sway or influence; a spirit; to supply with a source of power; ability to control or rule.*

The oppressors had demonic power to control others.

Hold it! Stop the presses! I just heard a knock at the door. It was a couple of solicitors from the local cult. Here I am writing a book on the anointing, and we're at a point discussing the power of the Anointed One and his anointing to break through deception, and two promoters of deception show up at the door.

Their opening line was to express a concern about stress affecting the family. I responded by explaining that the personal ministry of the Holy Spirit had already removed the burden of stress in my life. They then went into the need for individual peace, "which comes from your spirit." My response was that Jesus told us just before he left that he would leave his peace here for me, and that's what gives me my personal peace. Then I told them that they had come at a busy time for me because I was on the computer right in the middle of writing a book on the power of the Holy Spirit.

Suddenly, something very peculiar happened. The leader looked at me with a blank stare and stopped speaking. Can you imagine that? A speechless witness! A short time passed as I smiled and waited. Finally she said in a somewhat confused manner, "I have just completely lost my train of thought!" They excused themselves and walked away.

You see, deception cannot stand in the presence of the anointing of truth. As you learn to walk in the power of the anointing, don't be surprised when devils manifest. Use the spiritual discernment provided you by the Holy Spirit, respond in love to the people being deceived, and never forget your position of authority in the spirit realm.

Now back to Solomon:

> *This is an evil among all things that are done under the sun, that*
> *there is one event unto all: yea, also the heart of the sons of men is*
> *full of evil, and madness is in their heart while they live, and after*
> *that they go to the dead. (Ecclesiastes 9:3)*

Not much has changed, right? The heart of the sons of men is full of evil, and madness is in their heart while they live, and after that, they go to the dead. Besides the fact that the unsaved are going to hell in the end, do you think they might try to distribute a little hell while they're still here? After all, since they are the children of a *different* father, they are trying to fulfill their role here on earth as oppressors using the demonic power given to them by *their* father. Their system has certain similarities to our God's system, except it's the wrong team.

We don't deny the reality of their limited power. We don't even deny the legal right of Satan's crowd to present opportunities to oppress believers here in the earth realm. Remember, God's man Adam gave up the dominion he was given by God through disobedience. That's how the devil got his foot in the door. What we do deny is the right of the oppression to prevail against us. We refuse to grant it any victory. Just because we come across some oppression on the horizon of our lives, we are under no obligation to allow it to defeat us. That is the position Jesus restored for believers.

See Isaiah's comparison:

> *Because ye have said, We have made a covenant with death, and*
> *with hell are we at agreement; when the overflowing scourge shall*
> *pass through, it shall not come unto us: for we have made lies our*
> *refuge, and under falsehood have we hid ourselves. (Isaiah 28:15)*

Wow! What a level of deception! A covenant with death and with hell—are they in agreement! That's a pretty grim scenario for deceived mankind.

But God had a plan:

> *Therefore the redeemed of the LORD shall return, and come with singing unto Zion; and everlasting joy shall be upon their head: they shall obtain gladness and joy; and sorrow and mourning shall flee away. I, even I, am he that comforteth you: who art thou, that thou shouldest be afraid of a man that shall die, and of the son of man which shall be made as grass; And forgettest the LORD thy maker, that hath stretched forth the heavens, and laid the foundations of the earth; and hast feared continually every day because of the fury of the oppressor, as if he were ready to destroy? and where is the fury of the oppressor? (Isaiah 51:11-13)*

Everlasting joy shall be upon their heads, they shall obtain gladness and joy, and sorrow and mourning shall flee away. I, even I, am he that comforteth you—where is the fury of the oppressor? What a plan!

> *And all thy children shall be taught of the Lord; and great shall be the peace of thy children. In righteousness shalt thou be established: thou shalt be far from oppression; for thou shalt not fear: and from terror; for it shall not come near thee. (Isaiah 54:13)*

It doesn't sound like oppression is winning here, does it? I don't hear anybody crying.

In righteousness shall thou be established. Like a football player—fit, trained, down, set, ready for the next play, and fully prepared to take on the opposition.

> *No weapon that is formed against thee shall prosper; and every tongue that shall rise against thee in judgment thou shalt condemn. This is the heritage of the servants of the LORD, and their righteousness is of me, saith the LORD. (Isaiah 54:17)*

After Isaiah takes a couple chapters foretelling the coming of the Prince of Peace, God lets us in on some insights about the anointing that he will bring with him:

> *And it shall come to pass in that day, that his burden shall be taken away from off thy shoulder, and his yoke from off thy neck, and the yoke shall be destroyed because of the anointing. (Isaiah 10:27)*

There are a couple of very powerful spiritual principles here. First of all, it says, "And it shall come to pass *in that day.*" Isaiah is forecasting a specific day, a time when the fulfillment of this prophecy will manifest.

"That day" is quite important to us. It tells us that at a specific time, it will come to pass. We will see an anointing present in the Anointed One, which will remove burdens and destroy yokes.

In the following chapter, Isaiah continues to tell us about this special package of empowerments:

> *And the spirit of the LORD shall rest upon him, the spirit of wisdom and understanding, the spirit of counsel and might, the spirit of knowledge and of the fear of the LORD. (Isaiah 11:2)*

When Isaiah speaks of the coming of the Anointed One, he says the Spirit of the Lord shall rest upon him (the Holy Spirit), and then he begins to list various attributes of the anointing. Notice the manifestations of the anointing. They include wisdom, understanding, counsel, might, knowledge, and the fear of the Lord.

These are supernatural traits, giftings, and power from God the Father that come with the anointing.

In Isaiah chapter nine, the prophet describes the birth of the Prince of Peace. Verse two says that the people that walked in darkness have seen a great light. They that dwell in the land of the shadow of death, upon them hath the light shined. Verse four describes the breaking of the yoke and the burden of the oppressor. Verse six tells of his government and describes further the aspects of the Anointed One: Wonderful, Counselor, the Mighty God, the Everlasting Father, and the Prince of Peace. Of the increase of his government and peace there shall be no end.

Isaiah14:12 begins to describe the fall of Satan at the appearance of the Anointed One. The false pride of Satan is spoken of and, in verse sixteen, a nearly sarcastic comment about the enemy is made when the Word says, "Is *this* the man that made the earth to tremble, that did shake kingdoms?" While verse fifteen talks of the ultimate end of the enemy, we will see his fall as described by Jesus in Luke 10:

> *And he said unto them, I beheld Satan as lightning fall from heaven. (Luke 10:18)*

Isaiah 29:20 tells us that the terrible one is brought to naught. Chapter forty tells of the one who would precede the Anointed One; we know him as John the Baptist. Verse three describes him as the voice that cries in the wilderness.

In verses twenty-five through thirty-one we are told of the greatness of his might, strength, and power. Those verses tell us that he gives power to the faint; and to them that have no might he increases with strength.

Remember Solomon's observation about the oppressed?

> *I am thy God: I will strengthen thee; yea, I will help thee; yea, I will uphold thee with the right hand of my righteousness. (Isaiah 41:10-12)*

This is a clear reference to Jesus, the Anointed One, who sits at the right hand of the Father.

Isaiah continues to prophesy about the coming of the Anointed One:

> *Behold, my servant, whom I uphold; mine elect, in whom my soul delighteth; I have put my spirit upon him: he shall bring forth judgment to the Gentiles. He shall not cry, nor lift up, nor cause his voice to be heard in the street. A bruised reed shall he not break, and the smoking flax shall he not quench: he shall bring forth judgment unto truth. He shall not fail nor be discouraged, till he have set judgment in the earth: and the isles shall wait for*

his law. Thus saith God the Lord, *he that created the heavens, and stretched them out; he that spread forth the earth, and that which cometh out of it; he that giveth breath unto the people upon it, and spirit to them that walk therein: I the* Lord *have called thee in righteousness, and will hold thine hand, and will keep thee, and give thee for a covenant of the people, for a light of the Gentiles; To open the blind eyes, to bring out the prisoners from the prison, and them that sit in darkness out of the prison house. (Isaiah 42:1-7)*

God has Isaiah provide encouragement to us by clearly stating that He shall bring to pass the promise of the Coming One.

In Chapter fifty-five, He speaks of the fulfillment of the promise and the absolute surety of His word from heaven to come to pass in the earth:

For my thoughts are not your thoughts, neither are your ways my ways, saith the Lord. *For as the heavens are higher than the earth, so are my ways higher than your ways, and my thoughts than your thoughts. For as the rain cometh down, and the snow from heaven, and returneth not thither, but watereth the earth, and maketh it bring forth and bud, [(bear fruit], that it may give seed to the sower, and bread to the eater: So shall my word be that goeth forth out of my mouth: it shall not return unto me void, [without fruit], but it shall accomplish that which I please, and it shall prosper in the thing whereto I sent it. (Isaiah 55:8-11)*

The earth and the believer share something in common. The water sowed into the earth causes the earth to bring forth and produce fruit. The word sowed into the believer causes the believer to bring forth and produce fruit. Remember the manifestation of biblical fruit is what the walk of faith is all about.

Isaiah 61 foretells the details of the burden-removing and the yoke-destroying power of God—the anointing. (My translation shows the word *anointed* means empowered.)

The Spirit of the Lord GOD is upon me; because the LORD hath anointed me to preach good tidings unto the meek; he hath sent me to bind up the brokenhearted, to proclaim liberty to the captives, and the opening of the prison to them that are bound; To proclaim the acceptable year of the LORD, and the day of vengeance of our God; to comfort all that mourn; To appoint unto them that mourn in Zion, to give unto them beauty for ashes, the oil of joy for mourning, the garment of praise for the spirit of heaviness; that they might be called trees of righteousness, the planting of the LORD, that he might be glorified. (Isaiah 61:1-3)

But ye shall be named the Priests of the LORD: men shall call you the Ministers of our God. (Isaiah 61:6) (Paul will later call believers stewards of the anointing.)

The fulfillment of Isaiah's prophecies of the messenger, John the Baptist, are described in the book of John, chapter one:

But as many as received him, to them gave he power [the anointing] to become the sons of God, even to them that believe on his name. And the Word was made flesh, and dwelt among us, (and we beheld his glory, the glory as of the only begotten of the Father,) full of grace [supernatural empowerment] and truth [the Word]. (John 1:12,14)

And of his fulness have all we received, and grace for grace. For the law was given by Moses, but grace [supernatural empowerment] and truth [The Word] came by Jesus Christ [the Anointed One and his anointing]. No man hath seen God at any time; the only begotten Son, which is in the bosom of the Father, he hath declared him. And this is the record of John, when the Jews sent priests and Levites from Jerusalem to ask him, Who art thou? And he confessed, and denied not; but confessed, I am not the Christ [the Anointed One and his anointing]. He said, I am the voice of one crying in the wilderness, Make straight the way of the Lord, as said the prophet Esaias. (John 1:16-20)

Verse nineteen says this is the record of John. The Jews asked him, "Who are thou?"

John told them, "I am not the Christ, the Anointed One."

The familiar verse of the voice of one crying in the wilderness appears in verse twenty-three. As John's record continues, he says that he is to baptize with water. But there is one coming, the same is he, who baptizes as with fire and the Holy Spirit.

> *John answered them, saying, I baptize with water: but there standeth one among you, whom ye know not. (John 1:26)*

Verse thirty-two describes the Spirit descending like a dove, and it abode upon him.

> *And John bare record, saying, I saw the Spirit descending from heaven like a dove, and it abode upon him. (John 1:32)*

We're going to study this in detail later, but notice this: John has begun speaking about a transfer. The Spirit (with his anointing empowerments) transfers to Jesus, and then Jesus baptizes (transfers) believers with fire and the Holy Spirit. The flesh-and-blood man, Jesus of Nazareth, became empowered by the Holy Spirit of God the Father down here in this natural earth realm.

In Luke's account, beginning in chapter four, Jesus was full of the Holy Spirit and led by the Spirit into the wilderness. As Satan attempted to tempt (test, evaluate) Jesus in the wilderness for forty days, we can see very clearly the empowerment of the anointing. As Jesus loosed into the natural earth-realm the anointing by speaking the Word of God (truth), he was able to effectively resist the enemy, and Satan departed from him for a season.

> *And Jesus being full of the Holy Spirit returned from Jordan, and was led by the Spirit into the wilderness, being forty days tempted of the devil. And in those days he did eat nothing: and when they were ended, he afterward hungered. And the devil said unto him, If thou be the Son of God, command this stone that it be made bread. And Jesus answered him, saying, It is written, that man shall not live by bread alone, but by every word of God. And the devil, taking him up into an high mountain, shewed unto him*

all the kingdoms of the world in a moment of time. And the devil said unto him, All this power will I give thee, and the glory of them: for that is delivered unto me; and to whomsoever I will I give it. If thou therefore wilt worship me, all shall be thine. And Jesus answered and said unto him, Get thee behind me, Satan: for it is written, Thou shalt worship the Lord thy God, and him only shalt thou serve. And Jesus answered and said unto him, Get thee behind me, Satan: for it is written, Thou shalt worship the Lord thy God, and him only shalt thou serve. And he brought him to Jerusalem, and set him on a pinnacle of the temple, and said unto him, If thou be the Son of God, cast thyself down from hence: For it is written, He shall give his angels charge over thee, to keep thee: And in their hands they shall bear thee up, lest at any time thou dash thy foot against a stone. And Jesus answering said unto him, It is said, Thou shalt not tempt the Lord thy God. And when the devil had ended all the temptation, he departed from him for a season. And Jesus returned in the power of the spirit. He went into the synagogue on the sabbath day, and stood up for to read. (Luke 4:1-16)

This next text is parallel to Isaiah 61. It also describes the nature and attributes of the anointing, and the work that the anointing will accomplish in the life of the believer.

The Spirit of the Lord is upon me, because he hath anointed me to preach the gospel to the poor; he hath sent me to heal the broken-hearted, to preach deliverance to the captives, and recovering of sight to the blind, to set at liberty them that are bruised, to preach the acceptable year of the Lord . (Luke 4:18,19)

I like to call verses eighteen through nineteen **the Luke Four Checklist.** If you can find a burden or a yoke in your life that is described in the Luke Four Checklist, then there is a Word and an anointing for your particular circumstance. Imagine the punctuation placed just slightly differently, and apply it to your life:

The Spirit of the Lord is upon <u>me</u>, because he has anointed <u>me</u> to . . .

- *preach the gospel to the poor*
- *heal the brokenhearted*
- *preach deliverance to the captives*
- *preach recovering of sight to the blind*
- *to set at liberty them that are bruised*
- *to preach the acceptable year of the Lord*

Here's a special note for all you poverty-doctrine types: Jesus begins the Luke Four Checklist with a description of the anointing of increase as the Gospel teaches and reaches the poor, and then finishes with the acceptable year of the Lord, the debt-free lifestyle described in Leviticus 25, and the forgiveness of all debts. Here's what the Bible says about debts:

> *The LORD shall open unto thee his good treasure, the heaven to give the rain unto thy land in his season, and to bless all the work of thine hand: and thou shalt lend unto many nations, and thou shalt not borrow. (Deuteronomy 28:12)*

What part of *thou shalt not borrow* don't you understand? If you are truly operating in the anointing of increase and abundance, you won't need to borrow money from somebody else to meet your needs. We'll deal with scripturally based, debt-free living much more in my upcoming book on God's economic plan for the believer, *The Believer's Financial Workshop.*

Healing the brokenhearted, preaching deliverance to the captives, recovery of sight to the blind, and setting at liberty them that are bruised...brokenhearted can deal with every emotion, every aspect of your own personal baggage, all of the heartaches of failed relationships, family conflict, and every personality shortcoming. The deliverance of the captive: that's the drug addict and hooker being set free. No pattern of self-destructive behavior or addiction can stand in the face of the anointing.

The phrase "recovering of sight to the blind" does not limit the power of the anointing just to the restoration of physical sight.

It tells of an all-encompassing anointing to remove every burden and destroy every yoke as it applies to our natural body. No sickness, no disease, no symptom has a legal right to prevail in the presence of the Anointed One. The word *bruised* is best translated *crushed*, and describes the hopelessness, disillusionment, depression, and confusion of all who have reached bottom and are at the end of their emotional rope in this life. As Paul later describes these people, they are without Christ (the Anointed One and his anointing).

> *That at that time ye were without Christ, being aliens from the commonwealth of Israel, and strangers from the covenants of promise, having no hope, and without God in the world. (Ephesians 2:12)*

In other words, they are left to operate down here with only their own natural resources.

> *[Remember] that you were at that time separated (living apart) from Christ [excluded from all part in Him], utterly estranged and outlawed from the rights of Israel as a nation, and strangers with no share in the sacred compacts of the [Messianic] promise [with no knowledge of or right in God's agreements, His covenants]. And you had no hope (no promise); you were in the world without God. (Ephesians 2:12 AMP)*

Without God, there is no hope in the world. The anointing has been sown into the earth by a loving God for just those people—people who have no real hope for success in this world through their own natural resources.

If you can envision the traditional religious leaders of the day like ten pins in a bowling alley, Jesus literally knocks them out in verses twenty and twenty-one when he announces, "That day has come."

And he closed the book, and he gave it again to the minister, and sat down. And the eyes of all them that were in the synagogue were fastened on him. And he began to say unto them, This day is this scripture fulfilled in your ears. (Luke 4:20,21)

The appearance of the Anointed One, foretold by Isaiah and the prophets so long ago, is now here in the natural earth realm. And Jesus begins to fulfill his role on the world stage as the Anointed One in operation—and not just in title only. It is now that the burden-removing, yoke-destroying power of God through Christ will be distributed into the earth.

Some things never change, however. Just like the traditional denominational leaders of the day got angry when Jesus got the Holy Spirit, there are still some doing it today. I know of no quicker way to get the left foot of fellowship in some churches than to declare that the Holy One lives within you and empowers you.

And they were astonished at his doctrine: for his word was with power. And in the synagogue there was a man, which had a spirit of an unclean devil, and cried out with a loud voice, saying, Let us alone; what have we to do with thee, thou Jesus of Nazareth? art thou come to destroy us? I know thee who thou art; the Holy One of God. And Jesus rebuked him, saying, Hold thy peace, and come out of him. And when the devil had thrown him in the midst, he came out of him, and hurt him not. And they were all amazed, and spake among themselves, saying, What a word is this! for with authority and power he commandeth the unclean spirits, and they come out. And the fame of him went out into every place of the country round about. And he arose out of the synagogue, and entered into Simon's house. And Simon's wife's mother was taken with a great fever; and they besought him for her. And he stood over her, and rebuked the fever; and it left her: and immediately she arose and ministered unto them. Now when the sun was setting, all they that had any sick with divers diseases brought them unto him; and he laid his hands on every one of them, and healed them. And devils also came out of many, crying out, and saying, Thou art Christ the Son of God. And he rebuking them suffered them not to speak: for they knew that he was Christ [the Anointed One and His anointing]. (Luke 4:32-41)

Verse thirty-two says they were astonished at his doctrine because his word was with power (my study Bible defines *doctrine* as teaching):

- *For with authority and power he commandeth the unclean spirits, and they came out (verse 36)*
- *And he stood over her, and rebuked the fever; and it left her (verse 39)*
- *And he laid his hands on every one of them, and healed them (verse 40)*
- *And devils also came out of many crying out, and saying, thou art Christ [the Anointed One], the son of God (verse 41)*

And it came to pass on a certain day, as he was teaching, that there were Pharisees and doctors of the law sitting by, which were come out of every town of Galilee, and Judaea, and Jerusalem: and the power of the Lord was present to heal them. (Luke 5:17)

Remember Isaiah said the coming one would be revealed on a certain day.

This passage describes a typical "Jesus scene." We could word it this way today: "And it came to pass on a certain day as he was teaching, that all of the high-ranking religious leaders were gathered together—kind of like a denominational district meeting." All of the high muckety-mucks were there. You can just imagine the robes and the hats.

Okay, here comes a short rabbit trail. Let's face it, some denominations have the best hats. I saw a hat at a meeting one time that must have been nearly two feet tall. As one progresses in that particular denomination, the hats get better, richer, taller, more jewels inserted, and more gold. And the robes—my goodness!

Rich ladies at a New York dinner party in designer gowns don't have such a garment.

As was the case in those days, many religious leaders of today are more impressed with their own appearance and presence and their rank and status within their own denomination than they are with truly seeking and distributing the anointing to help the people.

Look at the unusual way God has the writer describe the presence of the anointing:

> *And the power of the Lord was present to heal them.*

Do you see in the historical biblical account that these self-centered, narrow-minded, religious leaders didn't receive a single thing from the Anointed One? There, sitting next to them, was the depository of the anointing here on earth and they got nothing—zip—nada. No faith, no transfer of the anointing, nothing. Contrast the attitude of indifference of these leaders with the persistence and focus of the men who brought their friend to the Anointed One and literally lowered their friend down through the roof to get to Jesus. No crowd, no traffic jam, and no reserved seating assignment could deter them.

> *And when he saw their faith (Luke 5:20)*

In verse twenty, a powerful spiritual principle is revealed to us: *And when He saw their faith.* Loosing our faith is required to touch the anointing. I appreciate Brother Kenneth Copeland's explanation of faith and the anointing working together like a two-part epoxy glue. The glue part is the anointing, and the hardener or catalyst is the faith of the believer. Neither part will do its assigned job without the other. Mix the two, faith and the anointing, and now you're doing business for God which will lead to manifestation.

And they were all amazed, and they glorified God, and were filled with fear, saying, We have seen strange things to day. (Luke 5:26)

The ones who witnessed the miraculous healing said, "We have seen strange things today." It was quite a debut for the Anointed One. "That day" had come.

This whole chapter was a summary of what God did in Christ, what Christ did to the devil, and what Christ did for certain people while he was down here on earth. Remember my previous mention of the "transfer"?

Next, we will deal with what Christ did in you, what we do to the devil, and what we do in the earth.

What a plan! Are you ready? Hang on to your seats!

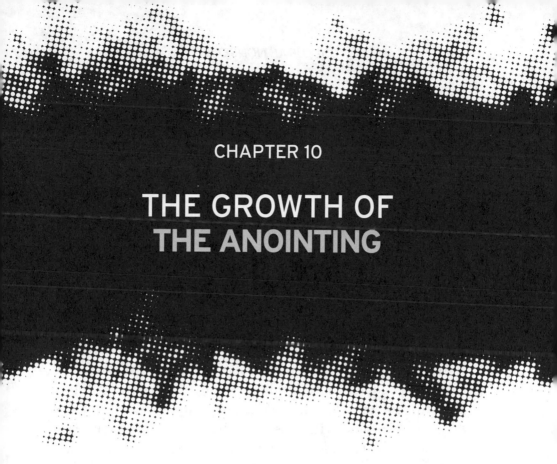

CHAPTER 10

THE GROWTH OF
THE ANOINTING

Jesus, the flesh-and-blood man from Nazareth, acknowledges the source of his empowerment:

Believest thou not that I am in the Father, and the Father in me? the words that I speak unto you I speak not of myself: but the Father that dwelleth in me, he doeth the works. (John 14:10)

Jesus said that his Father, who dwelled within him, did the works. And then he followed that statement with the promise that we shall do greater works. As the personal, present power of the Holy Spirit was manifested in the flesh-and-blood man Jesus, that empowerment will now begin to grow to inhabit countless millions of believers prepared to flow in the anointing given them by the Father.

In Acts 10, God communicates through visions and trances. As the opportunity to join the family of God expanded to the heathen Gentile nations, God granted a centurion a vision and instructed him to call on the man of God. At the same time, Peter fell into a heavy trance:

> *And he became very hungry, and would have eaten: but while they made ready, he fell into a trance. (Acts 10:10)*

God put the two men together to develop an evangelistic outreach to that heathen. Now picture this scene: Here is Peter the apostle sent to a group of people who were strangers to the covenant. Orthodox Jews were not even allowed to walk on the same side of the street with these people, let alone go into their houses. If you were born into the family, the children of Israel, you were in. You couldn't just decide to fill out a membership application to join the club. Why do you think they are so meticulous about their genealogy? This one begat that one, and that one begat the other one and on and on. Most of us quit with our grandmother's mother; that's about as far back as we can go.

Now here is the man of God preparing to explain the core message of the gospel. Do you imagine that he will begin to forecast the sequence of events of the end-time? I don't think so. Don't you think he was there to explain the basic, most important points of the faith? When he begins to open his mouth and give the message, he announces that God is no respecter of persons, the gospel message is now being offered to all of mankind, and no previous membership in the family of the children of Israel is required to begin fellowship with the Father through the Son. All prerequisites are gone.

This is a spectacular change in the relationship between God and man. This loving offer from the Creator now allows voluntary membership by choice and not by birthright! Jesus is now going to provide access to the Father for all mankind. As far as the religious leaders of the day were concerned, telling the Gentiles they could join the family amounted to religious treason, a revolution which needed to be squashed.

The status of the situation has changed. Instead of just the children of Israel being locked into that status for all their lives, now members of God's creation have the high privilege, by choice of their free moral will, to join the family of God. Jesus has come to set up a new plan. The people of the earth outside of the Jews can change teams. They get to pick their spiritual father. So after Jesus makes the offer, we have three groups remaining in the earth:

1.   God's creation (all those who have not yet accepted and confessed Christ)
2.   The Jews (who enjoy a certain special status, not quite the same as the creation and not quite the same as the Christian family)
3.   The children of the family of God (born-again Christian believers)

And just like a recent television commercial for a new credit card, membership does have its privileges. No membership equals no benefits. No wonder the first-century church with all its Jewish traditions had such a problem adjusting to these new members— these heathen dogs who were now in the family! This is an example of the loving God carrying free moral choice to its logical extreme; the offer is available to all. Whosoever will...

You can see how aggravating this must have been to the Jewish leaders. Now some of their main guys are inviting heathens to the secret meeting and giving away all of their private stuff. That's like giving away the confidential handshake down at the secret lodge meeting. Here are the guys with the big hats and robes from the big granite building downtown, and they are world-class upset.

Just a special note to those of you who are reading this book and are a member of a secret society: Here's a good opportunity for a simple loyalty test between your secret oaths and your faith in

God. Have you sworn not to disclose knowledge of ungodly things which have happened or are taught in the secret lodge meetings? Are there principles or rituals practiced which do not line up with the scriptures and glorify our God? Have you been asked to swear an allegiance or loyalty to one other than Christ? Or your spouse? Can you freely, openly, and transparently discuss the goals, objectives, procedures, and ceremonies of your secret club with your wife, fellow believers, or pastor?

I would just challenge you to submit your secretive and deceptive activities to the Holy Spirit for his correction or approval. I realize that some of the things you have been asked to swear to contain the threat of bodily harm should you elect to disclose them. As in most cults, your special status to do business with other cult members may be threatened.

Your continued participation in these things has two effects: first of all, your deception and secret activities will postpone the fulfillment of your true spiritual destiny as a believer; secondly, divided loyalty dilutes the mission of the church. However, you live in a day where there are many resources to assist you in getting set free. Specialized training books abound for dealing with cults and secret organizations. If these things exist in your life, I urge you to confront them and receive your deliverance and get on with the job which God has for you. After all, the anointing of Jesus is all about freedom and liberty.

Ordinary, uneducated believers were now speaking to the crowds, taking preeminence away from the religious leaders. Please notice that their only credentials were that they had been with Jesus. They had accepted the Anointed One and his anointing, and that was sufficient.

> Now when they saw the boldness and unfettered eloquence of Peter and John and perceived that they were unlearned and untrained in the schools [common men with no educational advantages], they marveled; and they recognized that they had been with Jesus. (Acts 4:13 AMP)

When you begin to flow in the anointing, some unusual circumstances may present themselves. I have been invited to teach in certain Bible colleges where I would not qualify to be a student; I don't meet their academic standards. Isn't God fun? Just go with the anointing and see where he takes you.

Now back to Peter:

> *How God anointed Jesus of Nazareth with the Holy Spirit and with power: who went about doing good, and healing all that were oppressed of the devil; for God was with him. (Acts 10:38)*

This verse declares the central core message of the New Testament Gospel and provides hope for all believers who daily confront oppression in their earthly lives.

God the Father placed his power in Jesus (the flesh-and-blood man from Nazareth) through the Holy Spirit (the anointing) and then commissioned him to go about doing good works. The Holy Spirit's empowerment was required to set people free from the oppression of the devil. Let all the earth rejoice! Praise the love of God for ever—he loves his people, and he wants them to be free! Set free by the love of God, set free by the anointing, every burden removed, and every yoke destroyed.

And yet if you ask the average sinner out there in the world, what is the core message of the church? Their answer would undoubtedly be, "If you don't behave, you're going to hell!" And immediately following would be some preacher's long list of things not to do—the don't do list. To the world, Christianity appears to be just a giant restriction on their fun and freedom. Instead of a message of liberty, the perception of our faith is just an updated list of laws and rules to fit the current culture. And then when some believer is caught in a failure to comply with these laws and rules, the church is judged by the culture to be a group of hypocrites. It is sad to think that the church has allowed the ungodly to define who we are as Christians, little anointed ones.

Because the most publicized message of the gospel is evangelistic in its nature, the message is always designed to contrast the new birth with whatever current sin is under discussion.

"We don't smoke and we don't chew and we don't go with girls that do."

The true core message of the Gospel is that there is a burden-removing, yoke-destroying power within you to set you free to live a holy life.

> *While Peter yet spake these words, the Holy Spirit fell on all them which heard the word. (Acts 10:44)*

And within a few short verses, while Peter yet spoke these words, the Holy Spirit fell on all that heard the word. And on the Gentiles also was poured out that gift of the Holy Spirit.

Now here's a good place to clear up an issue of doctrine. Did you notice that the hearers of the word who believed got the pouring out of the gift of the Holy Spirit **before** they got baptized in water? They even got filled before they confessed their sins to the priest. I understand that may be a problem for you because it's out of sequence from the way you may have been taught. Just stick with the Word and trust the Holy Spirit; it will all work out. Seek God and don't allow carnally minded people to make it a test of fellowship for you.

> I submit to you that when the Word says that he went about doing good, the description of those good works is not limited to just charitable works in the natural. As important as those good charitable works are, they do not require a supernatural empowerment—in other words, they don't require the anointing. I believe the flesh-and-blood man Jesus was empowered for supernatural works, as the historical account of the gospel confirms. Read it like this for that gospel perspective: *Who went about doing good (works which required the anointing).*

So the central message of the Gospel as described in Acts 10 is the fulfillment of the prophetic promises concerning the Anointed One.

In Acts 26, Jesus makes a personal visit to Saul, soon to become Paul, and outlines his ministry goals through the man of God. This personal visit to Paul on the Damascus Road gives him his goals, objectives, and Job description for his life-long ministry. The focus is on God's power and for believers to come out from under the devil's power.

> *But rise, and stand upon thy feet: for I have appeared unto thee*
> *for this purpose, to make thee a minister and a witness both of*
> *these things which thou hast seen, and of those things in the which*
> *I will appear unto thee; delivering thee from the people, and from*
> *the Gentiles, unto whom now I send thee, to open their eyes, and*
> *to turn them from darkness to light, and from the power of Satan*
> *unto God, that they may receive forgiveness of sins, and inher-*
> *itance among them which are sanctified by faith that is in me.*
> *(Acts 26:16-18)*

Believers were to learn from the ministry of Paul how to receive their inheritance. This would include every promise and covenant benefit entitled to them under this new arrangement between the Father and his new children, that new arrangement being that his creation could become members of the family through faith in the Son.

The short version of Jesus' instruction to Paul is quite simple: get them in the family, and teach them their inheritance. Show these new believers how to lay hold of their true covenant inheritance.

Doesn't this compare favorably with the precious vision described in the book of Isaiah?

> *And all thy children shall be taught of the LORD; and great shall*
> *be the peace of thy children. In righteousness shalt thou be estab-*
> *lished: thou shalt be far from oppression; for thou shalt not fear:*
> *and from terror; for it shall not come near thee. (Isaiah 54:13,14)*

Great shall be the peace of thy children. In righteousness you shall now be established. You shall be far from oppression.

Now there's a powerful word that benefits the whole family!

CHAPTER 11

YOUR LEAP
OF FAITH

J ust as Isaiah and Luke discussed this all-important issue of
their days, if the heart of the Gospel message is to manifest
in you, the question which you must answer is *when*, *how*
and *why* does that anointing manifest in you?

If you have truly accepted Christ, have you accepted the
Anointed One and his anointing? The present, personal ministry
of the Holy Spirit in our lives is to empower all believers, to anoint
them to fulfill the work they are called to do. This empowerment is
described in countless places in the scriptures, both old and new
covenants alike.

We have this treasure in earthen vessels—within us.

> *But we have this treasure in earthen vessels, that the excellency*
> *of the power may be of God, and not of us. (II Corinthians 4:7)*

However, we possess this precious treasure [the divine Light of the Gospel] in [frail, human] vessels of earth, that the grandeur and exceeding greatness of the power may be shown to be from God and not from ourselves. (II Corinthians 4:7 AMP)

We have been made partners in the anointing; partakers of the divine nature.

According as his divine power hath given unto us all things that pertain unto life and godliness, through the knowledge of him that hath called us to glory and virtue: Whereby are given unto us exceeding great and precious promises: that by these ye might be partakers of the divine nature, having escaped the corruption that is in the world through lust. (II Peter 1:3,4)

For His divine power has bestowed upon us all things that [are requisite and suited] to life and godliness, through the [full, personal] knowledge of Him Who called us by and to His own glory and excellence (virtue). By means of these He has bestowed on us His precious and exceedingly great promises, so that through them you may escape [by flight] from the moral decay (rottenness and corruption) that is in the world because of covetousness (lust and greed), and become sharers (partakers) of the divine nature. (II Peter 1:3,4 AMP)

John tells us we have this special impartation; that we have an *unction*, an anointing.

But ye have an unction from the Holy One, and ye know all things. But the anointing which ye have received of him abideth in you, and ye need not that any man teach you: but as the same anointing teacheth you of all things, and is truth, and is no lie, and even as it hath taught you, ye shall abide in him. (I John 2:20, 27)

Paul tells us that we have the internal power to see each of the Father's promises that we are to appropriate through our faith and the power of the anointing.

For all the promises of God in him are yea, and in him Amen, unto the glory of God by us. Now he which stablisheth us with you in Christ, and hath anointed us, is God; Who hath also sealed us, and given the earnest of the Spirit in our hearts. (II Corinthians 1:20-22)

Jesus acknowledged the Father's power at work in him saying, "It's not me who does the works, but my Father in me."

Believest thou not that I am in the Father, and the Father in me? the words that I speak unto you I speak not of myself: but the Father that dwelleth in me, he doeth the works. (John 14:10)

Do you not believe that I am in the Father, and that the Father is in Me? What I am telling you I do not say on My own authority and of My own accord; but the Father Who lives continually in Me does the (His) works (His own miracles, deeds of power). (John 14:10 AMP)

Luke clarifies the issue of the anointing in Acts 10:38:

How God anointed Jesus of Nazareth with the Holy Spirit and with power: who went about doing good, and healing all that were oppressed of the devil; for God was with him. (Acts 10:38)

How God anointed and consecrated Jesus of Nazareth with the [Holy] Spirit and with strength and ability and power; how He went about doing good and, in particular, curing all who were harassed and oppressed by [the power of] the devil, for God was with Him. (Acts 10:38 AMP)

See how God (the Heavenly Father) anointed Jesus of Nazareth (the flesh-and-blood man from Nazareth) with the Holy Spirit (the Spirit of God the Father) and with power (the anointing), who went about doing good (good works which require the anointing to perform) and healing (by supernatural means) all that were oppressed (remember Ecclesiastes 4:1) of the devil (the source of the oppression), for God was with him. (It's not me and you that are doing the works, but our Father in us!) Do you see it?

Acts 10:38

How God anointed
__Jesus of Nazareth__

with the Holy Spirit
and with power: who
went about doing
good, and healing all
that were oppressed
of the devil; for God
was with Him.

Acts 10:38

How God anointed

 David of Baltimore
Name/City

with the Holy Spirit
and with power: who
went about doing
good, and healing all
that were oppressed of
the devil; for God was
with him.

You fill in the blanks of this next form. Where do you stand?

Acts 10:38

How God anointed

_____

My Name/City

with the Holy Spirit and with power: who went about doing good, and healing all that were oppressed of the devil; for God was with _____.

him/her

These are holy documents demonstrating the progression of the anointing from God the Father to Jesus and then into the lives of believers. It is a divine transfer.

Anytime you fail to apply the anointing power to a given situation you will, by default, immediately fall back on limited natural human resources only. These include your earthly skill, intellect, strength, and self-discipline without the supernatural power of God. All you will have to depend on is in the natural.

I'm not that smart, well-educated, or skillful in manipulating all of the world systems and circumstances to depend on just my human resources. But you throw in the anointing, the favor of God, my contractual covenant benefits, and his promises taught in my Bible, and I am more than an overcomer, more than a conqueror, something which Paul talks about in the Bible. We get to that place where Paul tells us that he (the Father of the Son and the Holy Spirit in us) always causes us to triumph.

Remember this truth from Faith School: **The outcome of any situation is never determined by the totality of the power of God which is available. The outcome is set and limited only by what the believer is willing to accept.**

Oh man. I know that hurts. You're not the only one who lost a few battles in the war due to ignorance and unpreparedness.

> Is not this the Carpenter, the son of Mary and the brother of James and Joses and Judas and Simon? And are not His sisters here among us? And they took offense at Him and were hurt [that is, they disapproved of Him, and it hindered them from acknowledging His authority] and they were caused to stumble and fall. (Mark 6:3 AMP)

What happened that day in Nazareth? Did Jesus just have a bad day? The very presence of the Anointed One was in the earth and in his hometown to demonstrate its burden-removing, yoke-destroying power. Remember, the outcome of any situation is never determined by the totality of the power of God which is available. The outcome is set and limited only by what the believer is willing to accept.

THE PARABLE OF THE WITNESS STAND

God gave me a somewhat unique parable for describing my belief in the personal ministry of the Holy Spirit in my life and how that is in such direct contrast to how the natural, non-spiritual man thinks and lives. The story goes like this:

I am called by the court to appear as a witness in a case. After being sworn in by the bailiff, I take my position on the witness stand. After some preliminary questions, the district attorney begins to question me concerning my faith.

"Mr. MacDerment, based on your previous testimony, you have stated that you believe there is a spirit living inside you. Is that correct, Mr. MacDerment?"

"Yes, I believe the Holy Spirit of God dwells within me."

"And you further stated that you believe you receive council and direction from this spirit, is that correct?"

"Yes, that is correct."

"And you further stated that the very presence of this spirit inside you provides you with a ... some sort of supernatural power, is that correct?"

"Yes, you're starting to get the idea. That power you spoke of is the anointing."

"And you further stated that you believe it is the will of God for you to dispense this supernatural power according to his directions."

"Yes, that's how it works."

"Mr. MacDerment, don't you think it is a little confusing for us to understand this situation?"

"No it's not confusing to me at all. My brother and ministry partner Apostle Paul has made it very clear about understanding spiritual things. Any true understanding of these spiritual principles is exclusively reserved for those who are in Christ, the Anointed One, and his anointing. Receiving these eternal truths is for the Christian believer only. Sorry."

> *But of him are ye in Christ Jesus, who of God is made unto us wisdom, and righteousness, and sanctification, and redemption. (I Corinthians 1:30)*

> *But it is from Him that you have your life in Christ Jesus, Whom God made our Wisdom from God, [revealed to us a knowledge of the divine plan of salvation previously hidden]. (I Corinthians 1:30 AMP)*

> *But as it is written, Eye hath not seen, nor ear heard, neither have entered into the heart of man, the things which God hath prepared for them that love him. But God hath revealed them unto us by his Spirit: for the Spirit searcheth all things, yea, the deep things of God. (I Corinthians 2:9,10)*

> *But, on the contrary, as the Scripture says, What eye has not seen and ear has not heard and has not entered into the heart of man, [all that] God has prepared (made and keeps ready) for those who love Him [who hold Him in affectionate reverence, promptly obeying Him and gratefully recognizing the benefits He has bestowed]. [Isaiah 64:4; 65:17] Yet to us God has unveiled and revealed them by and through His Spirit, for the [Holy] Spirit searches diligently, exploring and examining everything, even sounding the profound and bottomless things of God [the divine counsels and things hidden and beyond man's scrutiny]. (I Corinthians 2:9,10 AMP)*

"And if you are not spiritually minded, it doesn't surprise me at all that you're unable to understand this."

> *But the natural man receiveth not the things of the Spirit of God: for they are foolishness unto him: neither can he know them, because they are spiritually discerned. (I Corinthians 2:14)*

> *But the natural, non-spiritual man does not accept or welcome or admit into his heart the gifts and teachings and revelations of the Spirit of God, for they are folly (meaningless nonsense) to him; and he is incapable of knowing them [of progressively recognizing, understanding, and becoming better acquainted with them] because they are spiritually discerned and estimated and appreciated. (I Corinthians 2:14 AMP)*

I continue to explain to the district attorney...

"You see, in your present state outside the family of God, it simply is not possible for you to understand this. You may observe its effects, like noticing the leaves moving because of the wind. You may observe a sick person who receives a healing, for example, at a Benny Hinn meeting. You may see the bondage of debt removed from a believer through the ministry of a man of God flowing in the debt-free anointing, like John Avanzini or Harold Herring from the Debt Free Army.

"You may observe someone who has been chronically insecure over his entire life now begin to exhibit confidence and contentment. The cravings of a drug addict may disappear, and he begins to live a normal life. Hookers may have a change of heart and come off the street and into a church.

"However, as a natural non-spiritual man, you're not wired to turn the light on. Without being born again and walking in the Spirit, you simply cannot understand.

"Let me explain what I mean by that. An electric wire goes to a switch and provides the power. The switch, when turned on, delivers the power to the light bulb, and the bulb does what it was created to do, bring forth light. I regret to tell you that unless you are a family member empowered by the Holy Spirit and in possession of revelatory knowledge and the faith to release it, you're not wired to turn the light bulb on. In your present spiritual condition, it is simply not possible for you to understand the ministry of the Holy Spirit. You're not in the family, and you're not entitled to know the family secrets. And God is under no obligation to reveal these things to you since you have no personal relationship with him.

"If you would like to join the family and learn more of the mysteries of the scripture, please meet with me privately immediately after the court session. I would love to have you as a brother (or sister) in the Lord and help you to begin your New Testament education.

"But, in the meantime, my appeal to you must be the same as the appeal of Jesus:

> Believe me that I am in the Father, and the Father in me: or else believe me for the very works' sake. (John 14:11)"

Many of the institutions of mankind are simply substitutes for the anointing. Consider medical care. When confronted with the physical ailment of a natural body, please cite for me an example where Jesus referred the patient to the nearby medical clinic. It's just not in there. The entire medical establishment is a substitute for the anointing. Isn't it interesting how quickly sick believers will so easily accept that God will work through doctors and medicine but wouldn't dare confess that their faith is sufficient to receive a supernatural healing?

I wonder where they learned that approach. Could this doctrine have come from somebody teaching from experience only? Because *he* didn't have the faith to be healed, he made a doctrine out of it and continues to teach from his experience of failure to obtain and not what the Word says. Oh, the traditions of men.

All of mankind is spirit being; that is our eternal nature. And I believe that within each spiritual being there is a vacuum that creates a strong hunger for something spiritual to fill the emptiness. That hunger must be filled. It will be filled with something. That vacancy in our spirit-man will either be filled by the truth from the Word of God and the leadership of his Holy Spirit through Jesus, or that vacancy will be filled by deception and the lies of the enemy—Satan and his demon forces…which leads me to another one of my favorite sayings:

People will believe anything.

Even if it's not the truth, they will believe *something*.

When a company is bought out by a larger firm and the truth is not presented to the employees, rumors, idle talk, and gossip surround the water cooler. The most outrageous speculation will be accepted as truth. The people will believe something, and if they are not offered the truth, they will believe anything.

Just look at today's contemporary, national, political dialogue. With all of the liars, deceivers, and thieves on the world stage today, and with the near-total absence of the truth, people will believe just about anything.

Talk about spiritual deception: do you remember the news story about a crazy cult in California? The leader had shaved his head and castrated himself, convinced all his followers that when a comet came by our earth, hidden behind the comet was the mother ship, a spaceship bus, that would take him and his followers off to an alien secret planet. Of course, the only way they could get to the secret planet was to drink the poisoned Kool-Aid. The end result was law enforcement officials finding dozens of dead bodies.

There is no doubt in my mind that those departed spirit-beings came in contact with the spirit that was providing the deception in the first place. Make no mistake about it, demonically inspired deception is a powerful force in this our earth, and people will believe anything if they are not provided with the truth.

Spiritualists, fortune-tellers, tea leaf readers, mediums, star-gazers, spell-casters, séances, astrologers, witches, spirit guides, channelers, necromancers—the problem is not whether they are real; they are real enough. The problem is they are all from the wrong team. They are from the devil and his crowd.

Let me tell you something that helped to establish the anointing at work in my life. I came home one evening after a church service, and upon exiting my truck I heard some unusual sounds, sort of like a slapping noise with crying and whimpering. I waited there in the dark for a moment, concentrating my senses on where the noises were coming from and trying to see what was going on.

As my vision adjusted to the darkness, I saw a neighbor two or three houses down, standing in his driveway, beating on his wife. She was crying but not really offering much resistance. He was holding her by the bathrobe with his left hand and slapping her in the face with his right.

Now I don't know what you would do. To what extent do you feel any obligation to intervene in a situation like this?

But as far as I was concerned, I was not going to let this jerk kill that woman if it was in my power to stop it. Recognizing the presence and power of God in my life has marked me. I now respond to challenges in a different way. Like any situation, my response must be in the spiritual realm as well as in the natural realm.

My first reaction was to immediately use the powerful name of Jesus and bind up the spirit of violence that was at work in that man. I also dispatched angels to surround the woman and to keep her safe from her attacker. Having faithfully responded in the spiritual realm first, my efforts could now be concentrated in the natural realm to safeguard her life. I could not tell if he had a knife or any other weapon. I moved closer toward the struggle while remaining in the shadows and darkness so as not to be observed and reveal my tactical position. My response in the natural included holding my mobile phone in one hand, ready to press the emergency 911 button, and my pistol in the other hand, ready to intervene if the situation deteriorated and her life appeared to be threatened.

We respond in the spiritual *and* in the natural.

Again, I don't know about you. You may not be a good one to have around in an emergency when the chips are down. But I knew one thing—I could stay just a spectator and watch this clown murder his wife and then later stand with her crying children at the gravesite. I could go into court to identify the killer, or I could do something before it happened.

As I drew closer, I noticed the noises had stopped. From my concealed position, I saw that the man had stopped slapping her and within seconds had begun crying and saying how sorry he was. They embraced each other and continued to sob and cry out loud. After a few convincing minutes, I withdrew unobserved back to my house. Mission accomplished. Praise God for the anointing. Praise God for his presence in my life.

Now whether she forgave him or insisted on counseling or called the sheriff's department the next morning, I don't know; that was up to her. But that experience for me was a powerful demonstration of God's presence in my life and helped me to take the leap of faith needed to recognize that and to willingly become a distributor of his anointing power.

What will motivate *you* to take that leap of faith?

What will it take to recognize the Anointed One and his anointing that resides in you?

What manner of man is this that even the winds and sea obey him? Sounds like a believer to me!

INFLUENCES OF THE BELIEVER

I have a soul (mind)

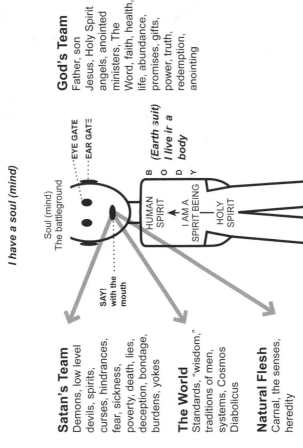

Soul (mind)
The battleground

EYE GATE
EAR GATE

God's Team
Father, son
Jesus, Holy Spirit
angels, anointed
ministers, The
Word, faith, health,
life, abundance,
promises, gifts,
power, truth,
redemption,
anointing

HUMAN
SPIRIT

I AM A
SPIRIT BEING

HOLY
SPIRIT

B
O
D
Y

(Earth suit)
I live in a
body

SAY!
with the
mouth

Satan's Team
Demons, low level
devils, spirits,
curses, hindrances,
fear, sickness,
poverty, death, lies,
deception, bondage,
burdens, yokes

The World
Standards, "wisdom,"
traditions of men,
systems, Cosmos
Diabolicus

Natural Flesh
Carnal, the senses,
heredity

A WORD TO THOSE WHO...AREN'T THERE YET

My brother and ministry partner Jerry Savelle has a wonderful saying. Jerry says, "Be ready to take your stand of faith forever, and you probably won't have to wait that long."

Boys and girls, just be ready to stand as long as it takes. Your loyalty to God and his Word is not dependent on the time spent believing God for something before you see a manifestation of that faith. Stand as long as it takes. You'll see the anointing do its work!

You must be hungry for the meat of God's Word or you wouldn't have read this far! Do you want to explore a little bit and see what may be holding you back from the anointing?

Study these scriptures for further revelation about the transfer of the anointing. For additional impact, try reading each one out of a complementary translation like the Amplified Bible or Message Bible.

Isaiah 10:27, 11:2
I John 2:20, 27
Acts 2:38, 3:5
John 14:10-12, 16-20
Romans 8:11, 15:13
Galatians 2:20, 3:5
Ephesians 1:19-20
I Corinthians 1:6, 2:5, 4:1, 6:19, 12:1-11
Colossians 1:27, 2:9-10
I Timothy 4:14
II Timothy 1:7, 14
II Corinthians 1:20-22, 2:14, 5:17, 6:16
Hebrews 2:4
James 4:7-8
I Peter 4:10
Philippians 1:19-20, 4:13,19
II Peter 1:4

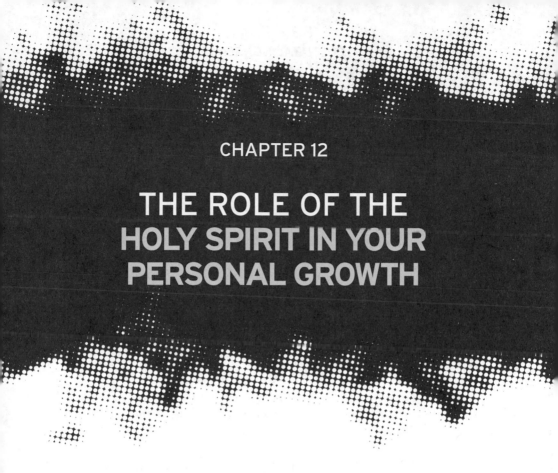

CHAPTER 12

THE ROLE OF THE HOLY SPIRIT IN YOUR PERSONAL GROWTH

This section is a general confidential survey to help you discover what may be holding you back from flowing in the anointing. Or, in other words, we're about to really get into your business!

> *In whom the god of this world hath blinded the minds of them which believe not, lest the light of the glorious gospel of Christ, who is the image of God, should shine unto them. (II Corinthians 4:4)*

> *For the god of this world has blinded the unbelievers' minds [that they should not discern the truth], preventing them from seeing the illuminating light of the Gospel of the glory of Christ (the Messiah), Who is the Image and Likeness of God. (II Corinthians 4:4 AMP)*

1. Has the Father given you the Comforter? What evidence have you experienced?

> *If ye love me, keep my commandments. And I will pray the Father, and he shall give you another Comforter, that he may abide with you for ever; even the Spirit of truth; whom the world cannot receive, because it seeth him not, neither knoweth him: but ye know him; for he dwelleth with you, and shall be in you. I will not leave you comfortless: I will come to you. (John 14:15-18)*

> *If you [really] love Me, you will keep (obey) My commands. And I will ask the Father, and He will give you another Comforter (Counselor, Helper, Intercessor, Advocate, Strengthener, and Standby), that He may remain with you forever—The Spirit of Truth, Whom the world cannot receive (welcome, take to its heart), because it does not see Him or know and recognize Him. But you know and recognize Him, for He lives with you [constantly] and will be in you. I will not leave you as orphans [comfortless, desolate, bereaved, forlorn, helpless]; I will come [back] to you. (John 14:15-18 AMP)*

2. Are you filled with the Holy Spirit? What evidence or manifestations have you experienced?

> *And I knew him not: but he that sent me to baptize with water, the same said unto me, Upon whom thou shalt see the Spirit descending, and remaining on him, the same is he which baptizeth with the Holy Spirit. (John 1:33)*

> *Then Peter said unto them, Repent, and be baptized every one of you in the name of Jesus Christ for the remission of sins, and ye shall receive the gift of the Holy Spirit. For the promise is unto you, and to your children, and to all that are afar off, even as many as the Lord our God shall call. (Acts 2:38,39)*

> *And Peter answered them, Repent (change your views and purpose to accept the will of God in your inner selves instead of rejecting it) and be baptized, every one of you, in the name of Jesus Christ for the forgiveness of and release from your sins; and*

you shall receive the gift of the Holy Spirit. For the promise [of the Holy Spirit] is to and for you and your children, and to and for all that are far away, [even] to and for as many as the Lord our God invites and bids to come to Himself. [Isaiah 57:19; Joel 2:32] (Acts 2:38,39 AMP)

But the fruit of the Spirit is love, joy, peace, longsuffering, gentleness, goodness, faith, meekness, temperance: against such there is no law. And they that are Christ's have crucified the flesh with the affections and lusts. If we live in the Spirit, let us also walk in the Spirit. (Galatians 5:22-25)

But the fruit of the [Holy] Spirit [the work which His presence within accomplishes] is love, joy (gladness), peace, patience (an even temper, forbearance), kindness, goodness (benevolence), faithfulness, gentleness (meekness, humility), self-control (self-restraint, continence). Against such things there is no law [that can bring a charge]. And those who belong to Christ Jesus (the Messiah) have crucified the flesh (the godless human nature) with its passions and appetites and desires. If we live by the [Holy] Spirit, let us also walk by the Spirit. [If by the Holy Spirit we have our life in God, let us go forward walking in line, our conduct controlled by the Spirit]. (Galatians 4:22-25 AMP)

3. Has he led you into any truth (revealed revelatory knowledge not obtained through natural resources)? Describe.

Howbeit when he, the Spirit of truth, is come, he will guide you into all truth: for he shall not speak of himself; but whatsoever he shall hear, that shall he speak: and he will shew you things to come. He shall glorify me: for he shall receive of mine, and shall shew it unto you. (John 16:13,14)

But when He, the Spirit of Truth (the Truth-giving Spirit) comes, He will guide you into all the Truth (the whole, full Truth). For He will not speak His own message [on His own authority]; but He will tell whatever He hears [from the Father; He will give the message that has been given to Him], and He will announce and declare to you the things that are to come [that will happen in the future]. He will honor and glorify Me, because He will take of (receive, draw upon) what is Mine and will reveal (declare, disclose, transmit) it to you. (John 16:13,14 AMP)

4. Do you set aside personal time to be in his presence? How often?

Blessed are they that keep his testimonies, and that seek him with the whole heart. (Psalm 119:2)

But without faith it is impossible to please him: for he that cometh to God must believe that he is, and that he is a rewarder of them that diligently seek him. (Hebrews 11:6)

But without faith it is impossible to please and be satisfactory to Him. For whoever would come near to God must [necessarily] believe that God exists and that He is the rewarder of those who earnestly and diligently seek Him [out]. (Hebrews 11:6 AMP)

Does your spouse set aside personal time to be in his presence? How often?

5. Have you ever "heard from God"? Has your spouse "heard from God"?

6. Has God ever used the Holy Spirit in you to manifest gifts of the Spirit? Has he used your spouse?

For I would that all men were even as I myself. But every man hath his proper gift of God, one after this manner, and another after that. (I Corinthians 7:7)

NOW ABOUT the spiritual gifts (the special endowments of supernatural energy), brethren, I do not want you to be misinformed. You know that when you were heathen, you were led off after idols that could not speak [habitually] as impulse directed and whenever the occasion might arise. Therefore I want you to understand that no one speaking under the power and influence of the [Holy] Spirit of God can [ever] say, Jesus be cursed! And no one can [really] say, Jesus is [my] Lord, except by and under the power and influence of the Holy Spirit. Now there are distinctive varieties and distributions of endowments (gifts, extraordinary powers distinguishing certain Christians, due to the power of divine grace operating in their souls by the Holy Spirit) and they vary, but the [Holy] Spirit remains the same. And there are distinctive varieties of service and ministration, but it is the same Lord [Who is served]. And there are distinctive varieties of operation [of working to accomplish things], but it is the same God Who inspires and energizes them all in all. But to each one is given the manifestation of the [Holy] Spirit [the evidence, the spiritual illumination of the Spirit] for good and profit. To one is given in and through the [Holy] Spirit [the power to speak] a message of wisdom, and to another [the power to express] a word of knowledge and understanding according to the same [Holy] Spirit; To another [wonder-working] faith by the same [Holy] Spirit, to another the extraordinary powers of healing by the one Spirit; To another the working of miracles, to another prophetic insight (the gift of interpreting the divine will and purpose); to another the ability to discern and distinguish between [the utterances of true] spirits [and false ones], to another various kinds of [unknown] tongues, to another the ability to interpret [such] tongues. All these [gifts, achievements, abilities] are inspired and brought to pass by one and the same [Holy] Spirit, Who apportions to each person individually [exactly] as He chooses. For just as the body is a unity and yet has many parts, and all the parts, though many, form [only] one body, so it is with Christ (the Messiah, the Anointed one). For by [means of the personal agency of] one [Holy] Spirit we were all, whether Jews or Greeks, slaves or free, baptized [and by baptism united together] into one body, and all made to drink of one [Holy] Spirit. (I Corinthians 12:1-13 AMP)

Which gifts have you seen manifested in your life by the power of the Holy Spirit:

*   Word of Knowledge
*   Word of Wisdom
*   Gift of Faith

- Gift of Healings
- Working of Miracles
- Gift of Prophesy
- Divers' Tongues
- Interpretation of Tongues
- Discerning of Spirits
- Spiritual Warfare
- Anointing of Might
- Anointing of Increase
- Spiritual Authority
- Other

7. Have you ever experienced supernatural peace during a critical situation?

Peace I leave with you, my peace I give unto you: not as the world giveth, give I unto you. Let not your heart be troubled, neither let it be afraid. (John 14:27)

Peace I leave with you; My [own] peace I now give and bequeath to you. Not as the world gives do I give to you. Do not let your hearts be troubled, neither let them be afraid. [Stop allowing yourselves to be agitated and disturbed; and do not permit yourselves to be fearful and intimidated and cowardly and unsettled]. (John 14:27 AMP)

8. Are you committed to operate in the supernatural anointing? Does your spouse have the same commitment? If not, why not? Could it be peer pressure (fear of man) not to? Do you just not want to stand out in the crowd?

9. Are you growing in your understanding that your personal supernatural anointing can and is to be applied to the everyday routine situations of your life?

10. Name what you believe to be the greatest hindrance to your personal spiritual growth.

Therefore if any man be in Christ, he is a new creature: old things are passed away; behold, all things are become new. (II Corinthians 5:17)

Therefore if any person is [ingrafted] in Christ (the Messiah) he is a new creation (a new creature altogether); the old [previous moral and spiritual condition] has passed away. Behold, the fresh and new has come! (II Corinthians 5:17 AMP)

Whatever your answer is here, you are the only one in charge of changing it!

The challenging questions contained in this survey were designed to prompt a meaningful self-examination. They should point out weaknesses and undergird strengths. There's no right or wrong answer, but your response should reveal a level of willingness to grow and progress in the things of God.

Just like changing one's abundance through the renewing of one's mind, developing a Word-inspired, Spirit-led lifestyle comes from seeking God over time. It just doesn't happen all at once. Step by step. Thought by thought. *Change comes at a pace and at a price.* Your quality decision to live a life for God is all encompassing; there's a lot to it.

Remember, when you serve an infinite God, you have a lot of homework to do. But, decision by decision, you mold and adjust your life's direction based on that inner vision—a vision birthed by the Word of God and the leadership of his Spirit. Anyway, you wouldn't be reading a study book like this if you weren't already seeking to progress on a godly path!

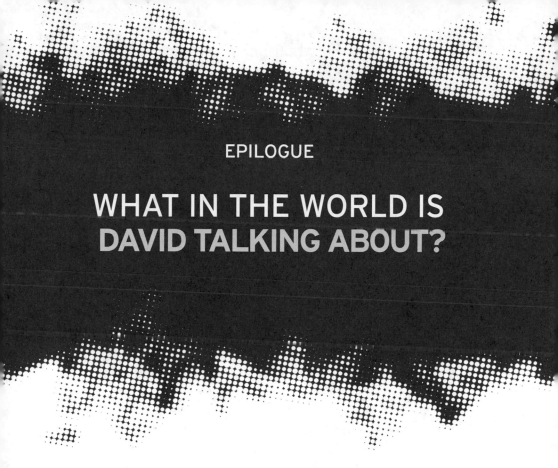

WHAT IN THE WORLD IS DAVID TALKING ABOUT?

INTERPRETIVE KEY TO MY FAVORITE SLOGANS

- **"Beverly-approved" story:** These stories have been submitted to my wife Beverly with the greatest latitude possible. She has determined them to be useful in training without being too crude, too extreme, or too "something that only David would relate to" and only this normal, well-grounded lady would understand.

- **If I was appointed the official commissar of the world for Christian education, I would require every believer to have a minimum of two years of gardening training.** Jesus said if you didn't understand Mark 4, you wouldn't get anything he was teaching. The cure for this problem is found in applying the basic principles of the walk of faith.

- **Everything you are believing for has to have a scriptural basis.** Boy, has this one saved me from going down a lot of time-wasting rabbit trails.

- **When you serve an infinite God, you have a lot of homework to do.** Isn't it amazing that some of you lazier members of the Christian family don't know much about our leader and his plan for you, and yet your entire future in this life and the next rests on your decisions concerning him and his plan?

- **Every experience is a learning experience.** This one comes from my father, a trained mechanical and industrial engineer and businessman. He was an incredibly methodical man. Every undertaking, whether small or large, required analysis, method, and a way to evaluate the results. He was big on quality control. If your efforts weren't producing the desired results, he had to conclude you were wasting time. All activities were broken down into step-by-step actions. We literally didn't wash the car without a written checklist. As an acute observer, he would constantly point out the cause-and-effect relationship between actions and results. To him, everything was a learning experience. Just riding to the grocery store was like a mini-course in the practical application of scientific principles. If we didn't learn something useful, we were just burning daylight.

- **Thank God there is a cure for ignorance.**
Remember, all ignorance is the absence of true
information. It just means that you missed that
class. With God, you can always make it up.
Remember the fellows who didn't know about
the Holy Spirit? (Acts 19:1-6; Acts 18:24-26; Acts
18:28)

- **I believe there is a word and an anointing for
every situation you face in life**. Now there's spiritual attitude for a "more than an overcomer" to
operate with. Anything less than that and you're
accusing Jesus of forgetting to take care of something while he was down here or neglecting to put
it in the operator's manual (the Word).

- **No message preached is worth much unless it
has manifested in the life of the speaker.** If the
modern, American, seminary-trained, denominational church had to comply with this principle,
most of them would shut down. This stuff is not
theory or third-party stories. The things of God
are real.

- **You are going to have to decide which horse
you are going to ride.** This is really a challenge to
the double-minded within the body of Christ. Do
you expect to see the divine, supernatural intervention of God in every situation of your life,
or do you just expect to get the same results the
world and the heathen and the untrained get?

- **Are you still suffering under the serious spiritual disadvantage of not having an Amplified
Bible?** I can see the nodding heads of the

serious students who quietly smile in agreement, thanking God for illumination which has come from their study in the Amplified Bible. I can also see the twisted faces of the poverty-doctrine types: Thirty dollars? I'm not paying thirty dollars for some book to read. Why, I'll just let that preacher do all of my homework for me.

- **People will believe anything.** I rest my case. If you have eyes and ears that work and have even the slightest level of Holy Spirit spiritual discernment working in your life, you have to admit that the spiritually deceived people of this demon-filled world will believe anything. If you don't get it, I really will pray for you.

CONFESSIONS AND DECLARATIONS FOR VICTORY

Targeting specific situations with the anointing

> **A General Declaration of Who I am in Christ:**
> **I am who God says I am.**
> **I can do what God says I can do.**
> **I can be what God says I can be.**
> **I can have what God says I can have.**

Taking authority over sleeplessness

"You low-level, tormenting devils, I take authority over you in the strong name of Jesus of Nazareth. I plead the blood of Jesus against you. The word of God says that when I resist you, you shall flee from me. In the name of Jesus, as it is written, so let it be done. Be gone and leave me alone. Now precious Holy Spirit, in faith I receive the peace that Jesus has given me."

Loosing the anointing against sickness

"You trespassing, microscopic organisms attempting to set up a stronghold of symptoms in my body, I curse you at the root, and I command you to dry up and die. Be removed and be cast into the sea in Jesus' name. Sickness and disease, you shall not lord it over me. Satan, you have no power or authority over me. Your attack on me shall not prevail. I plead the blood of Jesus against you, and I resist you. The Word of God says that when I resist you, you shall flee from me. As it is written, so let it be done in Jesus' name. Now precious Holy Spirit, by faith I loose that anointing within me to heal, to remove every burden and destroy every yoke. And by faith I receive my healing that Jesus provided for me on the cross 2,000 years ago."

Protecting your home and neighborhood by exercising your authority over the enemy

What weapons do you have and what resources can you draw on as a covenant believer? The name of Jesus, the blood of Jesus, the anointing of the Holy Spirit, mighty warring angels sent to labor on our behalf, anointing with oil, prayer cloths, etc. These are just some of your options. If you are at peace with these actions, then why don't you take these steps?

- Walk the boundaries of your property and reestablish that protective bloodline that Jesus bought, and don't allow the enemy to trespass into your blood-bought ground.

- Declare that God-given hedge of protection which surrounds your particular place of dominion. Reinforce the hedge with confessions of confidence in God's protecting power, and don't dismantle the hedge with confessions of fear, doubt, and unbelief.

- Take full authority over the neighborhood, and bind the demonic spirits in the powerful name of Jesus, the name which is above every name.

- Thank God for his covenant, where no evil shall befall me and no calamity shall come near my dwelling. He always causes us to triumph!

- Dispatch God's angels in the name of Jesus to go out and bring to pass the will of God.

Confess your faith in the keeping power of God's angels that watch over you and yours.

For the spouse who doesn't get it or doesn't want it

Stand your ground against the deceiving spirits which have blinded the eyes of men. Your best witness to those uncertain of the supernatural intervention of God is to demonstrate the manifestation of the promise. Remember the previously blind man's confession: "I was blind, but now I can see." Show the fruit and back it up with scripture and love. It cannot remain a doctrinal debate if that which was promised has now become real in your life. Case closed.

For those seeking a fuller measure of the Holy Spirit and the anointing. Filling is yielding. Spending time in the presence of God, studying his Word, walking out your covenant promises, speaking the Word over your life—all these personal commitments to the things of God draw you closer to him and the manifestation of the personal ministry of the Holy Spirit in your life.

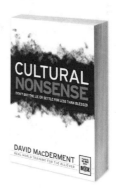

IF YOU'RE A FAN OF THIS BOOK, PLEASE TELL OTHERS...

- Write about *Cultural Nonsense* on your blog, Twitter, Myspace, or Facebook page.
- Suggest *Cultural Nonsense* to friends.
- When you're in a bookstore, ask them if they carry the book and if not, suggest that they order it.
- Write a review of *Cultural Nonsense* on www.amazon.com.
- Send me suggestions on websites, conferences, and events you know of where this book could be offered.
- Purchase additional copies to give away as gifts.

CONNECT WITH ME...

If you'd like to learn more about *Cultural Nonsense* please visit my website at www.culturalnonsense.com. I can also be contacted through email at david@culturalnonsense.com or mail at P.O. Box #90787, Lakeland, FL 33804.

David MacDerment is available for:

- **Real World Training Courses**—Instruction for the believer, available to churches and groups.

Can be adapted to various formats, seminars, etc. Training courses include in-depth studies on:

o   *Faith Which Produces Results*

o   *Answered Prayer*

o   *The Personal Ministry of the Holy Spirit*

o   *How to Obtain Healing*

o   *The Believer's Financial Workshop*—A biblical study of God's plan for His people; a strong contrast between the Scripture and the world's wisdom.

• **Conference Speaker**—Inspiring teaching that raises seekers up to a new level of the God kind-of-faith to believe for His promises.

• **Powerful Personal Testimony**—A moving story of personal victory through God's love and power.

• **Current Affairs and Relevant Issues for the Church**—Speaking and panel discussions of topics which challenge us all.